A GLOBAL SECURITY SYSTEM:
AN ALTERNATIVE TO WAR
EXECUTIVE SUMMARY

Resting on a convincing body of evidence that violence is not a necessary component of conflict among states and between states and non-state actors, World Beyond War asserts that war itself can be ended. We humans have lived without war for most of our existence and most people live without war most of the time. Warfare arose about 10,000 years ago (only five percent of our existence as Homo sapiens) and spawned a vicious cycle of warfare as peoples, fearing attack by militarized states, found it necessary to imitate them. So began the cycle of violence that has culminated in the last 100 years in a condition of permawar. War now threatens to destroy civilization as weapons have become ever more destructive. However, in the last 150 years, revolutionary new knowledge and methods of nonviolent conflict management have been developing that lead us to assert that it is time to end warfare and that we can do so by mobilizing millions around a global effort.

In this report you will find the pillars of war which must be taken down so that the whole edifice of the War System can collapse. Also in this report you will find the foundations of peace, already being laid, on which we will build a world where everyone will be safe. This report presents a comprehensive blueprint for peace as the basis of an action plan to finally end war.

It begins with a provocative "Vision of Peace" which may seem to some to be utopian until one reads the rest of the report which comprises the means for achieving it. The first two parts of the report present an analysis of how the current war system works, the desirability and necessity of replacing it, and an analysis of why doing this is possible. The next part outlines the Alternative Global Security System, rejecting the failed system of national security and replacing it with the concept of common security - **no one is safe until all are safe**. This system relies on three broad strategies for humanity to end war: 1) demilitarizing security, 2) managing conflicts without violence, and 3) creating a culture of peace. These are the strategies to dismantling the war machine and replacing it with a peace system that will provide a more assured common security. These comprise the "hardware" of creating a peace system. The next section, strategies for accelerating the already developing Culture of Peace, provides the "software," that is, the values and concepts necessary to operate a peace system and the means to spread them globally. The remainder of the report addresses realistic steps an individual or group can take, ending with a resource guide for further study.

While this report is based on the work of many experts in peace studies, political science, and international relations, as well as on the experience of many activists, it is intended to be an evolving plan as we gain more and more experience. The challenges outlined in the first part are real, interconnected, and tremendous. Sometimes we don't make the connections because we don't see them. Sometimes we simply bury our heads in the sand – the problems are too big, too overwhelming, too uncomfortable. The bad news is that the problems won't go away if we ignore them. The good news is that there is reason for *authentic hope*[1]. The historic end of war is now possible if we muster the will to act and so save ourselves and the planet from ever greater catastrophe. World Beyond War firmly believes that we can do this.

---

1. Peace activist and professor Jack Nelson-Pallmeyer coined the term "authentic hope" based on the premise that as individuals and collectively we are living in a difficult transition period marked by disruption and discontinuity. This period provides us with an opportunity and responsibility to shape the quality of our future. (Nelson-Pallmeyer, Jack. 2012. *Authentic Hope: It's the End of the World as We Know It, but Soft Landings Are Possible.* Maryknoll, N.Y.: Orbis Books.)

Main authors: Kent Shifferd; Patrick Hiller, David Swanson

Valuable feedback and/or contributions by: Russ Faure-Brac, Alice Slater, Mel Duncan, Colin Archer, John Horgan, David Hartsough, Leah Bolger, Robert Irwin, Joe Scarry, Mary DeCamp, Susan Lain Harris, Catherine Mullaugh, Margaret Pecoraro, Jewell Starsinger, Benjamin Urmston, Ronald Glossop, Robert Burrowes, Linda Swanson.

Apologies to those who have provided feedback and are not mentioned. Your input is valued.

Cover photo: James Chen; https://creativecommons.org/licenses/by-nc/4.0/legalcode.
The Wall, Israel, Bethlehem. Graf art sprayed on the Anti-terror wall by Palestinians ...
A wish for freedom.

Layout and design: Paloma Ayala www.ayalapaloma.com

PREFACE TO 2016 EDITION

Since its publication in March 2015, the World Beyond War "blueprint for ending war" titled *A Global Security System: An Alternative to War* – henceforth AGSS - has led to a lot of feedback – positive, negative, but mostly constructive. It became clear that this is not just another report, but a living document, a movement-building tool. We will continue to seek feedback for growth and improvement. The comments suggest that the report is a very useful tool to get people involved in World Beyond War, but more importantly it has inspired people to think about the larger vision of ending all war within the context of their work and has informed and educated them about the viable alternatives to war. All are elements which require a strategic plan for follow-up and continuation.

Why recurring editions?

The world does not stop when our booklet is published. Wars are still waged. In fact, according to the 2016 Global Peace Index, the world has become less peaceful and more unequal. There is work to be done, but we do not have to start from scratch.

By publishing revised editions of this report, we provide a mechanism for meaningful feedback as well as a sense of participation and ownership for contributors. We were able to highlight campaigns and developments and to interact with the readers and build community in our effort to create a world beyond war. We also know that we might not have sufficiently addressed all areas or that we simply failed to address an important perspective. On the positive side, through peace science and other contributions, new insights were developed which we now were able to integrate. With this report as an updated tool, there are opportunities for new presentations, new outreach, new partnerships. It is crucial to move beyond the choir with our efforts and connect the disconnected. World Beyond War and other movement builders can identify areas of focus based on developments highlighted in the report.

In preparing the 2016 edition of this report, we've listened to all feedback and integrated as much as possible. Some changes were small, others were simple updates based on new data available, and others were more significant. For example, we now emphasize the important role women play in preventing war and building peace at all levels and specifically point to the perils of patriarchy. Let's face it, even the norms of peace and security are male dominated. We have also added parts where we identify progress or setbacks. The 2015 U.S./Iran Nuclear Deal, for example, was a highly visible success story where diplomacy prevailed over war. The Catholic Church moved away from its "just war" doctrine and the Colombian Civil War has come to an end after 50 years.

TABLE OF CONTENTS

A VISION OF PEACE

We will know we have achieved peace when the world is safe for all the children. They will play freely out of doors, never worrying about picking up cluster bombs or about drones buzzing overhead. There will be good education for all of them for as far as they are able to go. Schools will be safe and free from fear. The economy will be healthy, producing useful things rather than those things which destroy use value, and producing them in ways that are sustainable. There will be no carbon-burning industry, and global warming will have been halted. All children will study peace and will be trained in powerful, peaceful methods of confronting violence, should it arise at all. They will all learn how to defuse and resolve conflicts peacefully. When they grow up they may enlist in a shanti sena, a peace force that will be trained in civilian-based defense, making their nations ungovernable if attacked by another country or a coup d'etat and therefore immune from conquest. The children will be healthy because health care will be freely available, funded from the vast sums that once were spent on the war machine. The air and water will be clean and soils healthy and producing healthy food because the funding for ecological restoration will be available from the same source. When we see the children playing we will see children from many different cultures together at their play because restrictive borders will have been abolished. The arts will flourish. While learning to be proud of their own cultures–their religions, arts, foods, traditions, etc.–these children will realize they are citizens of one small planet as well as citizens of their respective countries. These children will never be soldiers, although they may well serve humanity in voluntary organizations or in some kinds of universal service for the common good.

People can't work
for what they
can't imagine
(Elise Boulding)

INTRODUCTION: A BLUEPRINT FOR ENDING WAR

Whatever purpose the war system might once have served, it has now become dysfunctional to future human survival, yet it has not been abolished.

Patricia M. Mische (Peace Educator)

*I*n *On Violence*, Hannah Arendt wrote that the reason warfare is still with us is not a death wish of our species nor some instinct of aggression, ". . . but the simple fact that no substitute for this final arbiter in international affairs has yet appeared on the political scene."[1] The Alternative Global Security System we describe here is the substitute.

The goal of this document is to gather into one place, in the briefest form possible, everything one needs to know to work toward an end to war by replacing it with an Alternative Global Security System in contrast to the failed system of national security.

What is called national security is a chimerical state of things in which one would keep for oneself alone the power to make war while all countries would be unable to do so. . . . War is therefore made in order to keep or increase the power of making war.

Thomas Merton (Catholic Writer)

For nearly all of recorded history we have studied war and how to win it, but war has become ever more destructive and now threatens whole populations and planetary ecosystems with annihilation in a nuclear holocaust. Short of that, it brings "conventional" destruction unimaginable only a generation ago, while looming global economic and environmental crises go unattended. Unwilling to give in to such a negative end to our human story, we have begun to react in positive ways. We have begun to study war with a new purpose: to end it by replacing it with a system of conflict management that will result, at the very least, in a minimal peace. This document is a blueprint for ending war. It is not a plan for an ideal utopia. It is a summary of the work of many, based on many years of experience and analysis by people striving to understand why, when almost everyone wants peace, we still have wars; and on the work of countless people who have real-world political experience in nonviolent struggle as a substitute for war[2]. Many of these people have come together to work on World Beyond War.

1. Arendt, Hannah. 1970. *On Violence.* Houghton Mifflin Harcourt.

2. There now exists a large body of scholarship and a wealth of practical experience with creating institutions and techniques to manage conflict and practical experience with successful nonviolent movements, much of which is referenced in the resources section at the end of the *A Global Security System: An Alternative to War* document and on the World Beyond War website at www.worldbeyondwar.org.

The Work of World Beyond War

World Beyond War is helping build a global nonviolent movement to end war and establish a just and sustainable peace. We believe the time is right for a large-scale co-operation among existing peace and anti-war organizations and organizations seeking justice, human rights, sustainability and other benefits to humanity. We believe that the overwhelming majority of the world's people are sick of war and ready to back a global movement to replace it with a system of conflict management that does not kill masses of people, exhaust resources, and degrade the planet.

World Beyond War believes that conflict between nations and within nations will always exist and that it is all too frequently militarized with disastrous results for all sides. We believe that humanity can create – and already is in the process of creating – a non-militarized alternative global security system that will resolve and transform conflicts without resort to violence. We also believe that such a system will need to be phased in while militarized security is phased out; hence we advocate such measures as non-provocative defense and international peacekeeping in the early stages of the changeover.

We are confident that viable alternatives to war can and will be constructed. We do not believe we have described a perfect system. This is a work in progress which we invite others to improve. Nor do we believe that such an alternative system might not fail in limited ways. However, we are confident that such a system will not fail people in the massive ways that the current war system does, and we also provide means of reconciliation and a return to peace should such limited failures occur.

You will see here the elements of an Alternative Global Security System that does not rely on war or the threat of war. These elements include many for which people have long been working, sometimes for generations: the abolition of nuclear weapons, reform of the United Nations, ending the use of drones, changing national priorities from wars and preparations for war to meeting human and environmental needs, and many others. World Beyond War intends to cooperate fully with these efforts while mobilizing a mass movement to end war and replace it with an alternative global security system.

WHY IS AN ALTERNATIVE GLOBAL SECURITY SYSTEM BOTH DESIRABLE AND NECESSARY?

Photo: U.S. Department of Defense (www.defenselink. mil/; exact source) [Public domain], via Wikimedia Commons

The Iron Cage of War: The Present War System Described

When centralized states began to form in the ancient world, they were faced with a problem we have just begun to solve. If a group of peaceful states were confronted by an armed, aggressive war-making state, they had only three choices: submit, flee, or imitate the war-like state and hope to win in battle. In this way the international community became militarized and has largely remained so. Humanity locked itself inside the iron cage of war. Conflict became militarized. War is the sustained and coordinated combat between groups leading to large numbers of casualties. War also means, as author John Horgan puts it, militarism, the culture of war, the armies, arms, industries, policies, plans, propaganda, prejudices, rationalizations that make lethal group conflict not only possible but also likely[1].

In the changing nature of warfare, wars are not limited to states. One might speak of hybrid wars, where conventional warfare, terrorist acts, human rights abuses and other forms of large scale indiscriminate violence take place[2]. Non-state actors play an increasingly important role in warfare, which often takes the form of so-called asymmetric warfare.[3]

While particular wars are triggered by local events, they do not "break out" spontaneously. They are the inevitable result of a social system for managing international and civil conflict, the War System. The cause of wars in general is the War System which prepares the world in advance for particular wars.

Military action anywhere increases the threat of military action everywhere.

Jim Haber (Member of World Beyond War)

---

1. War Is Our Most Urgent Problem--Let's Solve It
(http://blogs.scientificamerican.com/cross-check/war-is-our-most-urgent-problem-let-8217-s-solve-it/)
2. Read more at: Hoffman, F. G. (2007). *Conflict in the 21st century: the rise of hybrid wars*. Arlington, Virginia: Potomac Institute for Policy Studies.
3. Asymmetric warfare takes place between fighting parties where relative military power, strategies or tactics differ significantly. Iraq, Syria, Afghanistan are the best known examples of this phenomenon.

The War System rests in part on a set of interlocked beliefs and values that have been around so long that their veracity and utility are taken for granted and they go mostly unquestioned, although they are demonstrably false.[4] Among common War System myths are:

- War is inevitable; we have always had it and always will.
- War is "human nature."
- War is necessary.
- War is beneficial.
- The world is a "dangerous place."
- The world is a zero-sum game (What you have I can't have and vice versa, and someone will always dominate; better us than "them.")
- We have "enemies."

We must abandon unexamined assumptions, e.g., that war will always exist, that we can continue to wage war and survive, and that we are separate and not connected.

Robert Dodge (Board Member, Nuclear Age Peace Foundation)

The War System also includes institutions and weapons technologies. It is deeply embedded in society and its various parts feed into each other so that it is very robust. For example, a handful of wealthy nations produce most of the weaponry used in the world's wars, and justify their own participation in wars on the basis of the damage done by weaponry they have sold or given to poor nations or groups.[5]

Wars are highly organized, preplanned mobilizations of forces prepared long in advance by the War System which permeates all institutions of society. For example, in the United States (a robust example of a war system participant), not only are there war-making institutions such as the executive branch of government where the head of state is also commander in chief, the military organization itself (Army, Navy, Air Force, Marine Corps, Coast Guard) and the CIA, NSA, Homeland Security, the several War Colleges, but war is also built into the economy, perpetuated culturally in the schools and religious institutions, a tradition carried on in families, glorified at sporting events, made into games and movies, and hyped by the news media. Almost nowhere does one learn of an alternative.

A single small example of just one pillar of the culture's militarism is military recruiting. Nations go to great lengths to enlist young people in the military, calling it "the Service." Recruiters go to great lengths to make "the Service" appear attractive, offering cash and educational inducements and portraying it as exciting and romantic. Never are the downsides portrayed. Recruiting posters do not show maimed and dead soldiers or blasted villages and dead civilians.

In the U.S., the Army Marketing and Research Group National Assets branch maintains a fleet of semi-trailer trucks whose highly sophisticated, attractive, interactive exhibits glorify warfare and are intended for recruiting in "hard to penetrate high schools." The fleet includes the "Army Adventure Semi", the "American Soldier Semi" and others.[6] Students can play in simulators and fight tank battles or fly Apache attack

---

4. *American Wars. Illusions and Realities* (2008) by Paul Buchheit clears up 19 misconceptions about U.S. wars and the U.S. war system. David Swanson's *War is a Lie* (2016) refutes 14 arguments used to justify wars.

5. For exact data on arms producers by nation, see the 2015 Stockholm International Peace Research Institute Yearbook chapter "International arms transfers and arms production" at https://www.sipri.org/yearbook/2015/10.

6. The Mobile Exhibit Company provides "an array of exhibits such as the Multiple Exhibit Vehicles, Interactive Semis, Adventure Semis, and Adventure Trailers manned by Army recruiters in order to re-connect America's People with America's Army and enhance Army awareness among high school and college students and their centers of influence. See the website at: http://www.usarec.army.mil/msbn/Pages/MEC.htm

helicopters and don Army gear for photo ops and get the pitch to join up. The trucks are on the road 230 days per year. The necessity of war is taken for granted and its destructive downside not exhibited. Photojournalist Nina Berman powerfully documented the U.S. Pentagon's self-promotion to the American public beyond the usual TV advertisements and presence at all sorts of sporting events.[7]

While wars are often launched or continued without majority public support, wars result in part from a certain, simple mindset. Governments have succeeded in convincing themselves and masses of people that there are only two responses to aggression: submit or fight - be ruled by "those monsters" or bomb them into the Stone Age. They frequently cite the "Munich Analogy," when in 1938 the British foolishly gave in to Hitler and then, eventually, the world had to fight the Nazis anyway. The implication is that had the British "stood up" to Hitler he would have backed down and there would have been no World War II. In 1939 Hitler attacked Poland and the British chose to fight. Tens of millions of people died.[8] A very hot "Cold War" with a nuclear arms race ensued. Unfortunately, in the 21st century, it has become patently clear that making war does not create peace, as the cases of the two Gulf Wars, the Afghan War and the Syrian/ISIS war clearly demonstrate. We have entered a state of permawar. Kristin Christman, in "Paradigm For Peace," suggests by way of analogy an alternative, problem-solving approach to international conflict:

> *We wouldn't kick a car to make it go. If something were wrong with it, we would figure out which system wasn't working and why: How is it not working? Does it turn on a little? Are the wheels spinning in mud? Does the battery need recharging? Are gas and air getting through? Like kicking the car, an approach to conflict that relies on military solutions does not figure things out: It does not distinguish between the causes of violence and does not address aggressive and defensive motivations.*[9]

We can end war only if we change the mindset, ask the relevant questions in order to get at the causes of an aggressor's behavior and, above all, to see if one's own behavior is one of the causes. Like medicine, treating only the symptoms of a disease will not cure it. In other words, we must reflect before pulling out the gun. This blueprint for peace does that.

The War System does not work. It does not bring peace, or even minimal security. What it produces is mutual insecurity. Yet we go on.

Wars are endemic; in a War System everyone has to beware of everyone else. The world is a dangerous place because the War System makes it so. It is Hobbes' "war of all against all." Nations believe they are victims of plots and threats by other nations, certain that the others' military might is aimed at their destruction, while failing to see their own failings, that their actions are creating the very behavior they fear and arm against, as enemies become mirror images of each other. Examples abound: the asymmetrical Arab-Israeli conflict, the India-Pakistan conflict, the American war on terror that creates ever more terrorists. Each side maneuvers for the strategic high ground. Each side demonizes the other while trumpeting its own unique contribution to civilization. Added to this volatility is the race for minerals, especially oil, as nations pursue an economic model of endless growth and addiction to oil[10]. Further, this situation of

Alternatives to particular wars are almost never seriously sought and the idea that there might be an alternative to War itself, almost never occurs to people.

---

7. The photo essay can be seen in the story "Guns and Hotdogs. How the U.S. Military Promotes its Weapons Arsenal to the Public" at https://theintercept.com/2016/07/03/how-the-us-military-promotes-its-weapons-arsenal-to-the-public/

8. Numbers vary greatly depending on source. Estimates range from 50 million to 100 million casualties, including the Pacific part of the war already underway.

9. *Paradigm for Peace* website: https://sites.google.com/site/paradigmforpeace/

10. A study found that foreign governments are 100 times more likely to intervene in civil wars when the country at war has large oil reserves. See an analysis and summary of the study in the *Peace Science Digest* at http://communication.warpreventioninitiative.org/?p=240

perpetual insecurity gives ambitious elites and leaders the opportunity to hold onto political power by fanning popular fears, and it provides tremendous opportunity for profit for arms makers who then support the politicians who fan the flames.[11]

In these ways the War System is self-fueling, self-reinforcing and self-perpetuating. Believing that the world is a dangerous place, nations arm themselves and act belligerently in a conflict, thus proving to other nations that the world is a dangerous place and that therefore they must be armed and act likewise. The goal is to threaten armed violence in a conflict situation in the hopes that it will "deter" the other side, but this fails on a regular basis, and then the goal becomes not to avoid a conflict, but to win it. Alternatives to particular wars are almost never seriously sought and the idea that there might be an alternative to War itself almost never occurs to people. One does not find what one does not seek.

It is no longer sufficient to end a particular war or particular weapons system if we want peace. The entire cultural complex of the War System must be replaced with a different system for managing conflict. Fortunately, as we shall see, such a system is already developing in the real world.

The War System is a choice. The gate to the iron cage is, in fact, open and we can walk out whenever we choose.

The Benefits of an Alternative System

The benefits are: no more mass killing and maiming, no more living in fear, no more grief from losing loved ones in wars, no more trillions of dollars wasted on destruction and preparing for destruction, no more pollution and environmental destruction that comes from wars and preparing for wars, no more war-driven refugees and war-induced humanitarian crises, no more erosion of democracy and civil liberties as government centralization and secrecy are rationalized by a war culture, no more maiming and dying from weapons left over from long ago wars.

> *The overwhelming majority of people from all cultures prefer to live in peace. At the deepest level of our being, people hate war. Whatever our culture, we share a desire for the good life, which most of us define as having a family, raising children and watching them grow into successful adults, and doing the work that we find meaningful. And war grotesquely interferes with those desires.*

Judith Hand (Author)

> *People choose for peace on the basis of their mental image of a possible and desirable future state of their living environment. This image can be as vague as a dream or as precise as a goal or mission statement. If peace advocates articulate a view of a realistic, credible and attractive future for people, a condition that is better in some ways than what now exists, then this image will be a goal that beckons and motivates people to pursue it. Not all people are enticed by the idea of peace.*

Luc Reychler (Peace Scientist)

11. In-depth sociological and anthropological evidence can be found in these books: Pilisuk, Marc, and Jennifer Achord Rountree. 2015. *The Hidden Structure of Violence: Who Benefits from Global Violence and War* Nordstrom, Carolyn. 2004. *Shadows of War: Violence, Power, and International Profiteering in the Twenty-First Century.*

Photos: Public Domain via WikiCommons

The Necessity of an Alternative System - War fails to bring peace

World War I was justified as the "war to end wars," but war never brings peace. It may bring a temporary truce, a desire for revenge, and a new arms race until the next war.

War is, at first, the hope that one will be better off; next the expectation that the other fellow will be worse off; then the satisfaction that he isn't any better off; and, finally, the surprise at everyone's being worse off."

Karl Kraus (Writer)

In conventional terms, the failure rate of war is fifty percent – that is, one side always loses. But in realistic terms, even the so-called victors take terrible losses.

Losses of war[12]

War	Casualties
World War II	Total - 50+ million Russia ("victor") - 20 million; U.S. ("victor") - 400,000+
Korean War	South Korea Military - 113,000 South Korea Civilian - 547,000 North Korea Military - 317,000 North Korea Civilian - 1,000,000 China - 460,000 U.S. Military - 33,000+
Vietnam War	South Vietnam Military - 224,000 North Vietnamese Military and Viet Cong - 1,000,000 outh Vietnamese Civilians - 1,500,000 North Vietnamese Civilians - 65,000; U.S. Military 58,000+

The casualties of war are far more than the actual dead. While there is controversy among those who try to measure war casualties, we warn against downplaying the numbers of civilian casualties, because that is a distraction from the long-lasting human costs of war. We propose that only a more integrative view of war casualties reflects the horrendous consequences. A thorough war casualty assessment must include direct and indirect war deaths. Indirect victims of war can be traced back to the following:

- Destruction of infrastructure
- Landmines
- Use of depleted uranium
- Refugees and internally displaced people
- Malnutrition
- Diseases
- Lawlessness
- Intra-state killings
- Victims of rape and other forms of sexual violence
- Social injustice

In June 2016, the United Nations High Commission on Refugees (UNHCR) stated that "wars and persecution have driven more people from their homes than at any time since UNHCR records began". At total of 65.3 million people were displaced at the end of 2015.[13]

---

12. Number can vary greatly depending on source. The website *Death Tolls for the Major Wars and Atrocities of the Twentieth Century* and the *Costs of War Project* were used to provide data for this table.

13. See http://www.unhcr.org/en-us/news/latest/2016/6/5763b65a4/global-forced-displacement-hits-record-high.html

Only by considering such "indirect" war casualties as actual casualties can the myth of "clean," "surgical" warfare with declining numbers of combat casualties be rightfully countered.

> *The havoc wreaked upon civilians is unparalleled, intended and unmitigated*

Kathy Kelly (Peace Activist)

Furthermore, in the late twentieth and early twenty-first centuries, wars seem not to end, but to drag on without resolution for years and even decades without peace ever being achieved. Wars do not work. They create a state of perpetual war, or what some analysts are now calling permawar. In the last 120 years the world has suffered many wars as the following partial list indicates:

> *the Spanish American War, the Balkan Wars, World War One, the Russian Civil War, the Spanish Civil War, World War Two, the Korean War, the Vietnam War, wars in Central America, the Wars of the Yugoslav Devolution, the First and Second Congo Wars, Iran-Iraq War, the Gulf Wars, the Soviet and U.S. Afghanistan wars, the U.S. Iraq war, the Syrian War, and various others including Japan versus China in 1937, long civil war in Colombia (ended in 2016), and wars in the Sudan, Ethiopia and Eritrea, the Arab-Israeli wars (a series of military conflicts between Israeli and various Arab forces), Pakistan versus India, etc.*

War is Becoming Ever More Destructive

The costs of war are immense on a human, social and economic level. Ten million died in World War I, 50 to 100 million in World War II. The war begun in 2003 killed five percent of the people in Iraq. Nuclear weapons could, if used, end civilization or even life on the planet. In modern wars it is not only soldiers that die on the battlefield. The concept of "total war" carried the destruction to non-combatants as well, so that today many more civilians— women, children, old men–die in wars than do soldiers. It has become a common practice of modern armies to indiscriminately rain high explosives on cities where large concentrations of civilians try to survive the carnage.

> *As long as war is looked upon as wicked, it will always have its fascination. When it is looked upon as vulgar, it will cease to be popular.*

Oscar Wilde (Writer and Poet)

War degrades and destroys the ecosystems upon which civilization rests. Preparation for war creates and releases tons of toxic chemicals. Most Superfund sites in the U.S. are on military bases. Nuclear weapons factories like Fernald in Ohio and Hanford in Washington State have contaminated ground and water with radioactive waste that will be poisonous for thousands of years. War fighting leaves thousands of square miles of land useless and dangerous because of landmines, depleted uranium weapons, and bomb craters that fill with water and become malaria infested. Chemical weapons destroy rainforest and mangrove swamps. The military forces use vast amounts of oil and emit tons of greenhouse gases.

In 2015, violence cost the world $ 13.6 trillion or $ 1,876 for every person in the world. This measure provided by the Institute of Economics and Peace in their 2016 Global Peace Index proves that economic losses "dwarf the expenditures and investments in peacebuilding and peacekeeping".[14] According to Mel Duncan, co-founder of the Nonviolent Peaceforce, the cost for a professional and paid unarmed civilian peacekeeper is $ 50,000 per year, compared to the $ 1 million it costs U.S. taxpayers for a soldier in Afghanistan per year.[15]

The World is Facing an Environmental Crisis

Humanity faces a global environmental crisis from which war both distracts us and which it exacerbates, including, but not limited to, adverse climate change which will disrupt agriculture, create droughts and floods, disrupt disease patterns, raise sea levels, set millions of refugees in motion, and disrupt natural ecosystems on which civilization rests. We must quickly shift the resources wasted in laying waste in the direction of addressing major problems humanity now faces.

Climate change, environmental degradation, and resource scarcity are contributing factors to war and violence. Some talk about a catastrophic convergence of poverty, violence, and climate change.[16] While we should not isolate those factors as causal drivers of war, they need to be understood as additional - and probably increasingly important - elements that are part of the social, political, and historical context of a war system.

It is necessary to interrupt this vicious path that is far more threatening to humans than the direct consequences of war. Starting with the military is a logical step. Not only does the out-of-control military budget take away much-needed resources for addressing the planetary crisis. The negative environmental impact of the military alone is tremendous.

The Institute for Economics and Peace, the National Priorities Project, Costs of War, the War Resisters League, the Stockholm International Peace Research Institute and others are doing invaluable work with regard to the absurd burden of war costs on the public.

---

14. See 2016 "Global Peace Index Report" at http://static.visionofhumanity.org/sites/default/files/GPI%20 2016%20Report_2.pdf

15. The estimated costs of soldier per year in Afghanistan range from $ 850,000 to $ 2.1 million depending on the source and year. See for example the report by the *Center for Strategic and Budgetary Assessments* at http:// csbaonline.org/wp-content/uploads/2013/10/Analysis-of-the-FY-2014-Defense-Budget.pdf or the report by the Pentagon comptroller at http://security.blogs.cnn.com/2012/02/28/one-soldier-one-year-850000-and-rising/. Regardless of the exact number, it is clear that it is exorbitant.

16. See: Parenti, Christian. 2012. *Tropic of Chaos: Climate Change and the New Geography of Violence.* New York: Nation Books.

Connecting the dots – illustrating the impact of war on the environment

- Military aircraft consume about one quarter of the world's jet fuel.
- The Department of Defense uses more fuel per day than the country of Sweden.
- The Department of Defense generates more chemical waste than the five largest chemical companies combined.
- A F-16 fighter bomber consumes almost twice as much fuel in one hour as the high-consuming U.S. motorists burn a year.
- The U.S. military uses enough fuel in one year to run the entire mass transit system of the nation for 22 years.
- During the 1991 aerial campaign over Iraq, the U.S. utilized approximately 340 tons of missiles containing depleted uranium (DU). There were significantly higher rates of cancer, birth defects and infant mortality in Fallujah, Iraq in in early 2010.[17]
- One military estimate in 2003 was that two-thirds of the Army's fuel consumption occurred in vehicles that were delivering fuel to the battlefield.[18]

In a report on the Post-2015 Development Agenda, the UN High-Level Panel of Eminent Persons made it clear that *business-as-usual* was not an option and that there needed to be transformative shifts including sustainable development and building peace for all.[19]

We simply can't go forward with a conflict management system that relies on war in a world that will have nine billion people by 2050, acute resource shortages and a dramatically changing climate that will disrupt the global economy and send millions of refugees on the move. If we do not end war and turn our attention to the global planetary crisis, the world we know will end in another and more violent Dark Age.

17. http://costsofwar.org/article/environmental-costs

18. Many works deal with the connections between war and the environment. Hastings in *American Wars. Illusions and Realities*: The Environmental Consequences of War are Insignificant; and Shifferd in *From War to Peace* provide very good overviews of the horrible consequences of war and militarism on the environment.

19. A New Global Partnership: Eradicate Poverty and Transform Economies through Sustainable Development. The Report of the High-Level Panel of Eminent Persons on the Post-2015 Development Agenda (http://www.un.org/sg/management/pdf/HLP_P2015_Report.pdf)

WHY WE THINK A PEACE SYSTEM IS POSSIBLE

Thinking that war is inevitable makes it so; it's a self-fulfilling prophecy. Thinking that ending war is possible opens the door to constructive work on an actual peace system.

There is already more Peace in the World than War

T The twentieth century was a time of monstrous wars, yet most nations did not fight other nations most of the time. The U.S. fought Germany for six years, but was at peace with the country for ninety-four years. The war with Japan lasted four years; the two countries were at peace for ninety-six.[1] The U.S. has not fought Canada since 1815 and has never fought Sweden or India. Guatemala has never fought France. The truth is that most of the world lives without war most of the time. In fact, since 1993, the incidence of interstate warfare has been declining.[2] At the same time, we acknowledge the changing nature of warfare as discussed previously. This is most notable in the vulnerability of civilians. In fact, the purported protection of civilians has been increasingly used as a justification for military interventions (e.g., the 2011 overthrow of the government of Libya).

We Have Changed Major Systems in the Past

Largely unanticipated change has happened in world history many times before. The ancient institution of slavery was largely abolished within less than a hundred years. Though significant new types of slavery can be found hiding in various corners of the earth, it is illegal and universally considered reprehensible. In the West, the status of women has improved dramatically in the last hundred years. In the 1950s and 1960s over a hundred nations freed themselves from colonial rule that had lasted centuries. In 1964 legal segregation was overturned in the U.S. In 1993, European nations created the European Union after fighting each other for over a thousand years. Difficulties like Greece's ongoing debt crisis or the 2016 Brexit vote - Britain leaving the European Union - are dealt with through social and political means, not through warfare. Some changes have been wholly unanticipated and have come so suddenly as to be a surprise even to the experts, including the 1989 collapse of the Eastern European communist dictatorships, followed in 1991 by the collapse of the Soviet Union. In 1994 we saw the end of apartheid in South Africa. 2011 saw the "Arab Spring" uprising for democracy catch most experts by surprise.

---

1. The U.S. has 174 bases in Germany and 113 in Japan (2015). These bases are widely considered "remnants" of World War II, but are what David Wine examines in his book *Base Nation*, showing the global base network of the U.S. as a questionable military strategy.

2. A comprehensive work on the decline of warfare: Goldstein, Joshua S. 2011. *Winning the War on War: The Decline of Armed Conflict Worldwide.*

We Live in a Rapidly Changing World

The degree and pace of change in the last hundred and thirty years is hard to comprehend. Someone born in 1884, potentially the grandparent of people now alive, was born before the automobile, electric lights, radio, the airplane, television, nuclear weapons, the internet, cell phones, and drones, etc. Only a billion people lived on the planet then. They were born before the invention of total war. And we are facing even greater changes in the near future. We are approaching a population of nine billion by 2050, the necessity of ceasing to burn fossil fuels, and a rapidly accelerating climate shift that will raise sea levels and flood coastal cities and low-lying areas where millions live, setting in motion migrations the size of which has not been seen since the fall of the Roman Empire. Agricultural patterns will change, species will be stressed, forest fires will be more common and widespread, and storms will be more intense. Disease patterns will change. Water shortages will cause conflicts. We cannot continue to add warfare to this pattern of disorder. Furthermore, in order to mitigate and adapt to the negative impacts of these changes we will need to find huge resources, and these can only come from the military budgets of the world, which today amount to two trillion dollars a year.

As a result, conventional assumptions about the future will no longer hold. Very large changes in our social and economic structure are beginning to occur, whether by choice, by circumstances we have created, or by forces that are out of our control. This time of great uncertainty has huge implications for the mission, structure and operation of military systems. However, what is clear is that military solutions are not likely to work well in the future. War as we have known it is fundamentally obsolete.

The Perils of Patriarchy are Challenged

Patriarchy, an age-old system of social organization that privileges masculine ways of conducting business, structuring laws, and guiding our lives, is proving to be perilous. The first signs of patriarchy were identified in the Neolithic Era, which lasted from about 10,200 BCE to between 4,500 and 2,000 BCE, when our early relatives relied on a system of divided labor whereby males hunted and females gathered to ensure the continuation of our species. Men are physically stronger and biologically predisposed to use aggression and domination to exert their will, we are taught, while women are more apt to use a "tend and befriend" strategy to get along socially.

Characteristics of patriarchy include dependence on hierarchy (power from the top down with one, or a privileged few, in control), exclusion (clear boundaries between "insiders" and "outsiders"), reliance on authoritarianism ("my way or the highway" as a common mantra), and competition (trying to get or win something by being better than others who want it also). This system privileges wars, encourages weapons gathering, creates enemies, and spawns alliances to protect the status quo.

Women and children are considered, too often, as underlings subservient to the will(s) of the older, wealthier, stronger male(s). Patriarchy is a way of being in the world that sanctions might over rights, resulting in resource plundering and redistribution by the top bidders. Value is too often measured by what goods, properties, and servants have been amassed rather than by the quality of human connections one cultivates. Patriarchal protocols and male ownership and control of our natural resources, our political processes, our economic institutions, our religious institutions, and our familial connections are the norm and have been throughout recorded history. We're led to believe that human nature is inherently competitive, and competition is what fuels capitalism, so capitalism must be the best economic system. Throughout recorded history women have largely been excluded from leadership roles, despite the fact that they

The bottom line is that cooperation and compassion are as much a part of the human condition as violence.

Photo: By FEMEN Women's Movement (Flickr: FEMEN against any form of Patriarchy) [CC BY-SA 2.0 (http://creativecommons.org/licenses/by-sa/2.0)], via Wikimedia Commons.

compromise half of the population who must abide by the laws the leaders impose. After centuries of rarely questioning beliefs that male forms of thought, body and social connection are superior to the female ones, a new era is in the offing. It is our collective task to advance the needed changes quickly enough to preserve our species and to provide a sustainable planet for future generations.

A good place to start shifting away from patriarchy is through early childhood education and the adoption of improved parenting practices, employing democratic rather than authoritarian guidelines in the growing of our families. Early education on non-violent communication practices and consensus decision-making would help prepare our youth for their roles as future policy makers. Success along these lines is already evidenced in numerous countries which have followed the compassionate principles of noted psychologist Marshall Rosenberg in the conducting of their national as well as international policies.

Education across all levels should encourage critical thinking and open minds instead of simply indoctrinating students to accept a status quo that fails to enrich personal well-being and to enhance overall societal health. Many countries offer free education because their citizens are viewed as human resources rather than as disposable cogs in corporate machinery. Investing in lifelong learning will lift all boats.

We need to critically examine the gendered stereotypes we've learned and to replace outdated biases with more nuanced thinking. Gender-bending fashion trends are blurring the binary gender categories of our past. If an era of enlightenment is at hand, we must be willing to alter our attitudes. More fluid gender identities are emerging, and that is a positive step.

We must discard the old-fashioned notion that genitalia have any impact on a person's value to society. Big strides have been made in breaking down gender barriers in occupations, earning potentials, recreational choices, and educational opportunities, but more must be done before we can assert that men and women are on equal footing.

We have already noticed changing trends in domestic life: there are now more singles than marrieds in the USA, and on average, women are marrying later in life. Women are less willing to identify as an adjunct to a dominant male in their lives, claiming their own identities instead.

Microloans are empowering women in countries with histories of misogyny. Educating girls is correlated with lowering birth rates and raising standards of living. Female genital mutilation is being discussed and challenged in areas of the globe where male control has always been the standard operating procedure. It has also been suggested, in following the example so recently set by Canada's new Prime Minister, Justin Trudeau, in his choosing to govern with a gender~balanced cabinet, that we should consider suggesting mandating, internationally, in all governments, the same parity not only for all elected offices but all civil servant positions as well. The progress on women's rights is substantial; achieving full equality with males will yield healthier, happier, and more robust societies.

Compassion and Cooperation are Part of the Human Condition

The War System is based on the false belief that competition and violence are the result of evolutionary adaptations, a misunderstanding of a popularization of Darwin in the nineteenth century which pictured nature as "red in tooth and claw" and human society as a competitive, zero-sum game where "success" went to the most aggressive and violent. But advances in behavioral research and evolutionary science show that

21

we are not doomed to violence by our genes, that sharing and empathy also have a solid evolutionary basis. In 1986 the Seville Statement on Violence (which refuted the notion of innate and inescapable aggression as the core of human nature) was released. Since that time there has been a revolution in behavioral science research which overwhelmingly confirms the Seville Statement.[3] Humans have a powerful capacity for empathy and cooperation which military indoctrination attempts to blunt with less than perfect success, as the many cases of post-traumatic stress syndrome and suicides among returning soldiers testify.

While it is true that humans have a capacity for aggression as well as cooperation, modern war does not arise out of individual aggression. It is a highly organized and structured form of learned behavior that requires governments to plan for it ahead of time and to mobilize the whole society in order to carry it out. The bottom line is that cooperation and compassion are as much a part of the human condition as violence. We have the capacity for both and the ability to choose either, but while making this choice on an individual, psychological basis is important, it must also lead to a change in social structures.

> *War does not go forever backwards in time. It had a beginning. We are not wired for war. We learn it.*

Brian Ferguson (Professor of Anthropology)

The Importance of Structures of War and Peace

It is not enough for the world's people to want peace. Most people do, but they nonetheless support a war when their nation state or ethnic group calls for it. Even passing laws against war, such as the creation of the League of Nations in 1920 or the famous Kellogg-Briand Pact of 1928 which outlawed war and was signed by the major nations of the world and never formally repudiated, did not do the job.[4] Both of these laudable moves were created within a robust War System and by themselves could not prevent further wars. Creating the League and outlawing war were necessary but not sufficient. What is sufficient is to create a robust structure of social, legal and political systems that will achieve and maintain an end to war. The War System is made up of such interlocked structures which make war normative. Therefore an Alternative Global Security System to replace it must be designed in the same interlocked way. Fortunately, such a system has been developing for over a century.

> *Almost nobody wants war. Almost everybody supports it. Why?*

Kent Shifferd (Author, Historian)

How Systems Work

Systems are webs of relationships in which each part influences the other parts through feedback. Point A not only influences point B, but B feeds back to A, and so on until points on the web are wholly interdependent. For example, in the War System, the military institution will influence education to set up Reserve Officers' Training Corps (ROTC) programs in the high schools, and the high school history courses will

---

3. The Seville Statement on Violence was designed by a group of leading behavioral scientists to refute "the notion that organized human violence is biologically determined". The entire statement can be read here: http://www.unesco.org/cpp/uk/declarations/seville.pdf

4. In *When the World Outlawed War* (2011), David Swanson shows how people around the world worked to abolish war, outlawing war with a treaty that is still on the books.

Photo: The United Nations as an example of global collaboration through supranational institutions.

present war as patriotic, inescapable and normative, while churches pray for the troops and parishioners work in the arms industry which Congress has funded in order to create jobs which will get Congress persons re-elected.[5] Retired military officers will head the arms manufacturing companies and get contracts from their former institution, the Pentagon. The latter scenario is what is infamously called the "military revolving door".[6] A system is made up of interlocked beliefs, values, technologies, and above all, institutions that reinforce each other. While systems tend to be stable for long periods of time, if enough negative pressure develops, the system can reach a tipping point and can change rapidly.

We live in a war-peace continuum, shifting back and forth between Stable War, Unstable War, Unstable Peace, and Stable Peace. Stable War is what we saw in Europe for centuries and now have seen in the Middle East since 1947. Stable Peace is what we have seen in Scandinavia for hundreds of years (apart from Scandinavian participation in U.S./NATO wars). The U.S. hostility with Canada which saw five wars in the 17th and 18th centuries ended suddenly in 1815. Stable War changed rapidly to Stable Peace. These phase changes are real world changes but limited to specific regions. What World Beyond War seeks is to apply phase change to the entire world, to move it from Stable War to Stable Peace, within and between nations.

> A global peace system is a condition of humankind's social system that reliably maintains peace. A variety of combinations of institutions, policies, habits, values, capabilities, and circumstances could produce this result. ... Such a system must evolve out of existing conditions.

Robert A. Irwin (Professor of Sociology)

An Alternative System is Already Developing

Evidence from archeology and anthropology now indicate that warfare was a social invention about 10,000 years ago with the rise of the centralized state, slavery and patriarchy. We learned to do war. But for over a hundred thousand years prior, humans lived without large-scale violence. The War System has dominated some human societies since about 4,000 B.C. But beginning in 1816 with the creation of the first citizen-based organizations working to end war, a string of revolutionary developments has occurred. We are not starting from scratch. While the twentieth century was the bloodiest on record, it will surprise most people that it was also a time of great progress in the development of the structures, values, and techniques that will, with further development pushed by nonviolent people power, become an Alternative Global Security System. These are revolutionary developments unprecedented in the thousands of years in which the War System has been the only means of conflict management. Today a competing system exists—embryonic, perhaps, but developing. Peace is real.

> Whatever exists is possible.

Kenneth Boulding (Peace Educator)

By the mid-nineteenth century the desire for international peace was developing rapidly. As a result, in 1899, for the first time in history, an institution was

---

5. See http://en.wikipedia.org/wiki/Reserve_Officers%27_Training_Corps for Reserve Officers Training Corps
6. There is ample research available in academic and reputable investigative journalism resources pointing to the revolving door. An excellent academic work is: Pilisuk, Marc, and Jennifer Achord Rountree. 2015. *The Hidden Structure of Violence: Who Benefits from Global Violence and War*

created to deal with global-level conflict. Popularly known as the World Court, the International Court of Justice exists to adjudicate interstate conflict. Other institutions followed rapidly including the first effort at a world parliament to deal with interstate conflict, the League of Nations. In 1945 the UN was founded, and in 1948 the Universal Declaration of Human Rights was signed. In the 1960s two nuclear weapons treaties were signed – the Partial Test Ban Treaty in 1963 and the Nuclear Non-Proliferation Treaty which was opened for signature in 1968 and went into force in 1970. More recently, the Comprehensive Test Ban Treaty in 1996, the landmines treaty (Antipersonnel Landmines Convention) in 1997, and in 2014 the Arms Trade Treaty were adopted. The landmine treaty was negotiated through unprecedented successful citizen-diplomacy in the so-called "Ottawa Process" where NGOs together with governments negotiated and drafted the treaty for others to sign and ratify. The Nobel Committee recognized the efforts by International Campaign to Ban Landmines (ICBL) as a "convincing example of an effective policy for peace" and awarded the Nobel Peace Prize to ICBL and its coordinator Jody Williams.[7]

The International Criminal Court was established in 1998. Laws against the use of child soldiers have been agreed on in recent decades.

Nonviolence: The Foundation of Peace

As these were developing, Mahatma Gandhi and then Dr. Martin Luther King Jr. and others developed a powerful means of resisting violence, the method of nonviolence, which has now been tested and found successful in many conflicts in different cultures around the world. Nonviolent struggle changes the power relationship between oppressed and oppressor. It reverses seemingly unequal relationships, as for example in the case of the "mere" shipyard workers and the Red Army in Poland in the 1980s (the Solidarity Movement led by Lech Walesa ended the repressive regime; Walesa ended up as president of a free and democratic Poland), and in many other cases. Even in the face of the what is considered one of the most dictatorial and evil regimes in history - the German Nazi regime - nonviolence showed successes on different levels. For example, in 1943 Christian German wives launched a nonviolent protest until almost 1,800 imprisoned Jewish husbands were released. This campaign now is commonly known as the Rossenstrasse Protest. On a larger scale, the Danes launched a five-year campaign of nonviolent resistance to refuse to assist the Nazi war machine using nonviolent means and subsequently saving Danish Jews from being sent to concentration camps.[8]

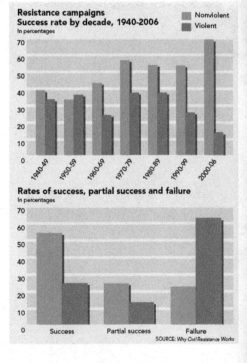

Resistance campaigns
Success rate by decade, 1940-2006
In percentages
■ Nonviolent
■ Violent

Rates of success, partial success and failure
In percentages

SOURCE: *Why Civil Resistance Works*

Nonviolence reveals the true power relationship, which is that all governments rest on the consent of the governed and that consent can always be withdrawn. As we shall see, continuing injustice and exploitation change the social psychology of the conflict situation and thus erode the will of the oppressor. It renders oppressive governments helpless and makes the people ungovernable. There are many modern instances of the successful use of nonviolence. Gene Sharp writes:

> *A vast history exists of people who, refusing to be convinced that the apparent 'powers that be' were omnipotent, defied and resisted powerful rulers, foreign conquerors, domestic tyrants, oppressive systems, internal usurpers and economic masters. Contrary to usual perceptions, these means of struggle by protest, noncooperation and disruptive intervention have played major historical roles in all parts of the world. . . .*[9]

Erica Chenoweth and Maria Stephan have demonstrated statistically that from 1900 to 2006, nonviolent resistance was twice as successful as armed resistance and resulted in more stable democracies with less chance of reverting to civil and international

---

7. See more on the ICBL and citizen diplomacy in *Banning Landmines: Disarmament, Citizen Diplomacy, and Human Security* (2008) by Jody Williams, Stephen Goose, and Mary Wareham.

8. This case is well documented in the Global Nonviolent Action Database (http://nvdatabase.swarthmore.edu/content/danish-citizens-resist-nazis-1940-1945) and the documentary series *A Force More Powerful* (www.aforcemorepowerful.org/).

9. See Gene Sharp's (1980) *Making the abolition of war a realistic goal*

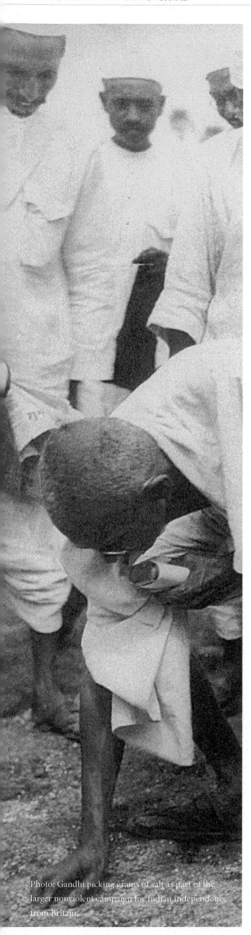

Photo: Gandhi picking grains of salt as part of the larger nonviolent campaign for Indian independence from Britain.

violence. In short, nonviolence works better than war.[10] Chenoweth was named one of the 100 Top Global Thinkers by Foreign Policy in 2013 "for proving Gandhi right." Mark Engler and Paul Engler's 2016 book *This Is An Uprising: How Nonviolent Revolt Is Shaping the Twenty-First Century* surveys direct action strategies, bringing out many of the strengths and weaknesses of activist efforts to effect major change in the United States and around the world since well before the twenty-first century. This book makes the case that disruptive mass movements are responsible for more positive social change than is the ordinary legislative "endgame" that follows.

Nonviolence is a practical alternative. Nonviolent resistance, coupled with strength-ened institutions of peace, now allows us to escape from the iron cage of warfare into which we trapped ourselves six thousand years ago.

Other cultural developments also contributed to the growing movement toward a peace system including the powerful movement for women's rights (including educating girls), and the appearance of tens of thousands of citizen groups dedicated to working for international peace, disarmament, strengthening international peace-making and peacekeeping institutions. These NGOs are driving this evolution toward peace. Here we can mention only a few such as the Fellowship of Reconciliation, Women's International League for Peace and Freedom, the American Friends Service Committee, the United Nations Association, Veterans for Peace, the International Campaign to Abolish Nuclear Weapons, the Hague Appeal for Peace, the Peace and Justice Studies Association and many, many others easily found by an internet search. World Beyond War lists on its website hundreds of organizations and thousands of individuals from all over the world who have signed our pledge to work to end all war.

Both governmental and non-governmental organizations began peacekeeping inter-vention, including the UN's Blue Helmets and several citizen-based, nonviolent ver-sions such as the Nonviolent Peaceforce and Peace Brigades International. Churches began to develop peace and justice commissions. At the same time there was a rapid spread of research into what makes for peace and a rapid spread of peace education at all levels. Other developments include the spread of peace-oriented religions, the de-velopment of the World Wide Web, the impossibility of global empires (too costly), the end of de facto sovereignty, the growing acceptance of conscientious objection to war, new techniques of conflict resolution, peace journalism, the development of the global conference movement (gatherings focusing on peace, justice, the environment, and development)[11], the environmental movement (including the efforts to end reliance on oil and oil-related wars), and the development of a sense of planetary loyalty.[12][13] These are only a few of the significant trends that indicate a self-organizing, Alternative Global Security System is well on the way to development.

10. Chenoweth, Erica, and Maria Stephan. 2011. *Why Civil Resistance Works: The Strategic Logic of Nonviolent Conflict.*

11. In the past twenty-five years there have been seminal gatherings at the global level aimed at creating a peaceful and just world. This emergence of the global conference movement, initiated by the Earth Summit in Rio de Janeiro in Brazil in 1992, laid the foundations for the modern global conference movement. Focused on environment and development, it produced a dramatic shift toward the elimination of toxins in production, the development of alternative energy and public transportation, reforestation, and a new realization of the scarcity of water. Examples are: Earth Summit Rio 1992 on the environment and sustainable development; Rio+20 brought together thousands of participants from governments, the private sector, NGOs and other groups, to shape how humans can reduce poverty, advance social equity and ensure environmental protection on an ever more crowded planet; Triennial World Water Forum as the largest international event in the field of water to raise awareness on water issues and solutions (initiated 1997); The Hague Appeal for Peace Conference of 1999 as the largest international peace conference by civil society groups.

12. These trends are presented in-depth in the study guide "The Evolution of a Global Peace System" and the short documentary provided by the War Prevention Initiative at http://warpreventioninitiative.org/?page_id=2674

13. A 2016 survey found that almost half of the respondents across 14 tracking countries considered themselves more global citizens than citizens of their country. See Global Citizenship A Growing Sentiment Among Citizens Of Emerging Economies: Global Poll at http://globescan.com/news-and-analysis/press-releases/press-releases-2016/103-press-releases-2016/383-global-citizenship-a-growing-sentiment-among-citizens-of-emerging-economies-global-poll.html

OUTLINE OF AN ALTERNATIVE GLOBAL SECURITY SYSTEM

No single strategy will end war. Strategies must be layered and woven together to be effective. In what follows, each element is stated as concisely as possible. Entire books have been written about each of them, a few of which are listed in the resources section. As will be apparent, choosing a world beyond war will require us to dismantle the existing War System and create the institutions of an Alternative Global Security System and/or to further develop those institutions where they already exist in embryo. Note that World Beyond War is not proposing a sovereign world government but rather a web of governing structures voluntarily entered into and a shift in cultural norms away from violence and domination.

Common Security

Conflict management as practiced in the iron cage of war is self-defeating. In what is known as the "security dilemma," states believe they can only make themselves more secure by making their adversaries less secure, leading to escalating arms races that culminated in conventional, nuclear, biological and chemical weapons of horrific destructiveness. Placing the security of one's adversary in danger has not led to security but to a state of armed suspicion, and as a result, when wars have begun, they have been obscenely violent. Common security acknowledges that one nation can only be secure when all nations are. The national security model leads only to mutual insecurity, especially in an era when nation states are porous. The original idea behind national sovereignty was to draw a line around a geographical territory and control everything that attempted to cross that line. In today's technologically advanced world that concept is obsolete. Nations cannot keep out ideas, immigrants, economic forces, disease organisms, information, ballistic missiles, or cyber-attacks on vulnerable infrastructure like banking systems, power plants, stock exchanges. No nation can go it alone. Security must be global if it is to exist at all.

Demilitarizing Security

Conflicts typical of the contemporary world cannot be resolved at gunpoint. They require not a recalibration of military tools and strategies but a far-reaching commitment to demilitarization.

Tom Hastings (Author and Professor of Conflict Resolution)

Shift to a Non-Provocative Defense Posture

A first step toward demilitarizing security could be non-provocative defense, which is to reconceive and reconfigure training, logistics, doctrine, and weaponry so that a nation's military is seen by its neighbors to be unsuitable for offense but clearly able to mount a credible defense of its borders. It is a form of defense that rules out armed attacks against other states.

> *Can the weapon system be effectively used abroad, or can it be only used at home? If it can be used abroad, then it is offensive, particularly if that 'abroad' includes countries with which one is in conflict. It if can only be used at home then the system is defensive, being operational only when an attack has taken place.[1]*

(Johan Galtung, Peace and Conflict Researcher)

Non-provocative defense implies a truly defensive military posture. It includes radically reducing or eliminating long-range weapons such as Intercontinental Ballistic Missiles, long-range attack aircraft, carrier fleets and heavy ships, militarized drones, nuclear submarine fleets, overseas bases, and possibly tank armies. In a mature Alternative Global Security System, a militarized non-provocative defense posture would be gradually phased out as it became unnecessary.

Another defensive posture that will be necessary is a system of defense against futuristic attacks including cyber-attacks on the energy grid, power plants, communications, financial transactions and defense against dual-use technologies such as nanotechnology and robotics. Ramping up the cyber capabilities of Interpol would be a first line of defense in this case and another element of an Alternative Global Security System.[2]

Also, non-provocative defense would not rule out a nation having long-range aircraft and ships configured exclusively for humanitarian relief. Shifting to non-provocative defense weakens the War System while making possible the creation of a humanitarian disaster relief force that strengthens the peace system.

Create a Nonviolent, Civilian-Based Defense Force

Gene Sharp has combed history to find and record hundreds of methods that have been used successfully to thwart oppression. Civilian-based defense (CBD)

> *indicates defense by civilians (as distinct from military personnel) using civilian means of struggle (as distinct from military and paramilitary means). This is a policy intended to deter and defeat foreign military invasions, occupations, and internal usurpations.[3] This defense "is meant to be waged by the population and its institutions on the basis of advance preparation, planning, and training.*
>
> *It is a "policy [in which] the whole population and the society's institutions become the fighting forces. Their weaponry consists of a vast variety*

---

1. This statement by Johan Galtung is put into context by himself, when he suggests that defensive weapons are still highly violent, but that there is reason to be optimistic that such a path of transarmament from conventional military defense will develop into nonviolent non-military defense. See complete paper at: https://www.transcend.org/galtung/papers/Transarmament-From%20Offensive%20to%20Defensive%20Defense.pdf

2. Interpol is the International Criminal Police Organization, set up in 1923, as an NGO facilitating international police cooperation.

3. Sharp, Gene. 1990. Civilian-Based Defense: A Post-Military Weapons System. Link to entire book: http://www.aeinstein.org/wp-content/uploads/2013/09/Civilian-Based-Defense-English.pdf

of forms of psychological, economic, social, and political resistance and counter-attack. This policy aims to deter attacks and to defend against them by preparations to make the society unrulable by would-be tyrants and aggressors. The trained population and the society's institutions would be prepared to deny the attackers their objectives and to make consolidation of political control impossible. These aims would be achieved by applying massive and selective noncooperation and defiance. In addition, where possible, the defending country would aim to create maximum international problems for the attackers and to subvert the reliability of their troops and functionaries.

Gene Sharp (Author, Founder of Albert Einstein Institution)

The dilemma faced by all societies since the invention of war, namely, to either submit or become a mirror image of the attacking aggressor, is solved by civilian-based defense. Becoming as or more war-like than the aggressor was based on the reality that stopping him requires coercion. Civilian-based defense deploys a powerful coercive force that does not require military action.

In civilian-based defense, all cooperation is withdrawn from the invading power. Nothing works. The lights don't come on, or the heat, the waste is not picked up, the transit system doesn't work, courts cease to function, the people don't obey orders. This is what happened in the "Kapp Putsch" in Berlin in 1920 when a would-be dictator and his private army tried to take over. The previous government fled, but the citizens of Berlin made governing so impossible that, even with overwhelming military power, the takeover collapsed in weeks. All power does not come from the barrel of a gun.

In some cases, sabotage against government property would be deemed appropriate. When the French Army occupied Germany in the aftermath of World War I, German railway workers disabled engines and tore up tracks to prevent the French from moving troops around to confront large-scale demonstrations. If a French soldier got on a tram, the driver refused to move.

Two core realities support civilian-based defense; first, that all power comes from below—all government is by consent of the governed and that consent can always be withdrawn, causing the collapse of a governing elite. Second, if a nation is seen as ungovernable, because of a robust civilian-based defense force, there is no reason to try to conquer it. A nation defended by military power can be defeated in war by a superior military power. Countless examples exist. Examples also exist of peoples rising up and defeating ruthless dictatorial governments through nonviolent struggle, beginning with the liberation from an occupying power in India by Gandhi's people power movement, continuing with the overthrow of the Marcos regime in the Philippines, the Soviet-backed dictatorships in Eastern Europe, and the Arab Spring, to name only a few of the most notable examples.

In a civilian-based defense all able adults are trained in methods of resistance.[4] A standing Reserve Corps of millions is organized, making the nation so strong in its independence that no one would think of trying to conquer it. A CBD system is widely publicized and totally transparent to adversaries. A CBD system would cost a fraction of the amount now spent to fund a military defense system. CBD can provide effective defense within the War System, while it is an essential component of a robust peace system. Certainly one can argue that nonviolent defense must transcend the

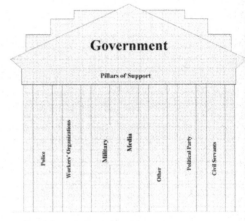

Graphic: Pillars of support for government. From the Book *On Strategic Nonviolent Conflict: Thinking About The Fundamentals* By The Albert Einstein Institution p.171 (http://www.aeinstein.org/wp-content/uploads/2013/09/OSNC.pdf)

---

4. See Gene Sharp, *The Politics of Nonviolent Action* (1973), *Making Europe Unconquerable* (1985), and *Civilian Based Defense* (1990) among other works. One booklet, *From Dictatorship to Democracy* (1994) was translated into Arabic prior to the Arab Spring.

nation-state view as forms of social defense, since the nation state itself often is an instrument of oppression against physical or cultural existence of peoples.[5]

As noted above, scientifically proven wisdom holds that nonviolent civil resistance is twice as likely to be successful compared to movements that use violence. The contemporary knowledge in theory and practice is what makes longtime nonviolent movement activist and scholar George Lakey hopeful for a strong role of CBD. He states: "If the peace movements of Japan, Israel and the United States choose to build on a half century of strategy work and devise a serious alternative to war, they will certainly build in preparation and training and gain the attention of pragmatists in their societies."[6]

Phase Out Foreign Military Bases

In 2009 the U.S. lease on an air base in Ecuador was set to expire and the president of Ecuador made a proposal to the U.S.

> *We'll renew the base on one condition: that they let us put a base in Miami.*

The British people would find it unthinkable if their government allowed Saudi Arabia to establish a large military base in the British Isles. Similarly, the United States would not tolerate an Iranian air base in Wyoming. These foreign establishments would be seen as a threat to their security, their safety and their sovereignty. Foreign military bases are valuable for controlling populations and resources. They are locations from which the occupying power can strike inside the "host" country or against nations on its borders, or possibly deter attacks. They are also frightfully expensive for the occupying country. The United States is the prime example, having hundreds of bases in 135 countries around the world. The actual total seems to be unknown; even Defense Department figures vary from office to office. Anthropologist David Vine, who has extensively researched the presence of U.S. military bases all over the world, estimates that there are 800 locations that station troops globally. He documents his research in the 2015 book *Base Nation. How U.S. military bases abroad harm America and the world.* Foreign bases create resentment against what is seen locally as imperial domination.[7] Eliminating foreign military bases is a pillar of an Alternative Global Security System and goes hand-in hand with non-provocative defense.

Withdrawing to an authentic defense of a nation's borders is a key part of demilitarizing security, thus weakening the ability of the War System to create global insecurity. As an alternative, some of the bases could be converted to civilian use in a "Global Aid Plan" as country assistance centers (see below). Others could be converted to solar panel arrays and other systems of sustainable energy.

Disarmament

Disarmament is an obvious step leading toward a world beyond war. The problem of war is in great measure a problem of wealthy nations flooding poor nations with weapons, most of them for a profit, others for free. Regions of the world that we think of as war-prone, including Africa and most of Western Asia, do not manufacture most

Photo: Armed Predator drone firing Hellfire missile

5. See Burrowes, Robert J. 1996. *The Strategy of Nonviolent Defense: A Gandhian Approach* for a comprehensive approach to nonviolent defense. The author considers CBD strategically flawed.

6. See George Lakey "Does Japan really need to expand its military to solve its security dilemma?" http://wagingnonviolence.org/feature/japan-military-expand-civilian-based-defense/

7. Osama bin Laden's stated reason for his horrific terrorist attack on the World Trade Center was his resentment against American military bases in his home country of Saudi Arabia.

of their own weapons. They import them from distant, wealthy nations. International small arms sales, in particular, have skyrocketed in recent years, tripling since 2001.

The United States is the world's leading weapons seller. Most of the rest of international weapons sales come from the four other permanent members of the United Nations Security Council plus Germany. If these six countries stopped dealing weapons, global disarmament would be a very long way toward success.

The violence of poor countries is often used to justify war (and arms sales) in wealthy countries. Many wars have U.S.-made weapons on both sides. Some have U.S. trained and armed proxies on both sides, as has been the case lately in Syria where troops armed by the Department of Defense have fought troops armed by the CIA. The typical response is not disarmament, but more armament, more weapons gifts and sales to proxies, and more arms purchases in the wealthy nations.

The United States is not just the biggest arms seller, but also the biggest arms buyer. Were the United States to scale back its arsenal, removing various weapons systems that lack a defensive purpose, for example, a reverse arms race might be kick started.

Efforts to end war are crippled by the ongoing existence and growth of the arms trade, but scaling back and ending the arms trade is a possible path toward ending war. Strategically, this approach has some possible advantages. For example, opposing U.S. weapons sales to Saudi Arabia or gifts to Egypt or Israel does not require a confrontation with U.S. patriotism in the way that opposing U.S. wars does. Instead we can confront the arms trade as the global health threat that it is.

Disarmament will require reductions in so-called conventional weapons as well as nuclear and other weapons types. We will need to end profiteering in arms trading. We will need to restrain the aggressive pursuit of global dominance that leads other nations to acquire nuclear weapons as deterrents. But we will also need to take on disarmament step-by-step, eliminating particular systems, such as armed drones, nuclear, chemical, and biological weapons, and weapons in outer space.

Conventional Weapons

The world is awash in armaments, everything from automatic weapons to battle tanks and heavy artillery. The flood of arms contributes both to the escalation of violence in wars and to the dangers of crime and terrorism. It aids governments that have committed gross human rights abuses, creates international instability, and perpetuates the belief that peace can be achieved by guns.

The United Nations Office for Disarmament Affairs (UNODA) is guided by the vision of promoting global norms of disarmament and oversees efforts to deal with weapons of mass destruction and conventional arms and the arms trade.[8] The office promotes nuclear disarmament and non-proliferation, strengthening of the disarmament regimes in respect to other weapons of mass destruction, and chemical and biological weapons, and disarmament efforts in the area of conventional weapons, especially landmines and small arms, which are the weapons of choice in contemporary conflicts.

---

8. See UNODO website at http://www.un.org/disarmament/

Outlaw the Arms Trade

Arms manufacturers have lucrative government contracts and are even subsidized by them and also sell on the open market. The U.S. and others have sold billions in arms into the volatile and violent Middle East. Sometimes the arms are sold to both sides in a conflict, as in the case of Iraq and Iran and the war between them that killed between 600,000 and 1,250,000 based on scholarly estimates.[9] Sometimes weapons end up being used against the seller or its allies, as in the case of weapons the U.S. provided to the Mujahedeen which ended up in the hands of al Qaeda, and the arms the U.S. sold or gave to Iraq which ended up in the hands of ISIS during its 2014 invasion of Iraq.

The international trade in death-dealing weapons is huge, over $70 billion per year. The main exporters of arms to the world are the powers that fought in World War II; in order: U.S., Russia, Germany, France, and the United Kingdom.

The UN adopted the Arms Trade Treaty (ATT) on April 2, 2013. It does not abolish the international arms trade. The treaty is an "instrument establishing common international standards for the import, export and transfer of conventional arms." It entered into force in December 2014. In the main, it says the exporters will monitor themselves to avoid selling arms to "terrorists or rogue states." The U.S., which has not ratified the treaty, nonetheless made certain that it had a veto over the text by demanding that consensus govern the deliberations. The U.S. demanded that the treaty leave huge loopholes so that the treaty will not "unduly interfere with our ability to import, export, or transfer arms in support of our national security and foreign policy interests" [and] "the international arms trade is a legitimate commercial activity" [and] "otherwise lawful commercial trade in arms must not be unduly hindered." Further, "There is no requirement for reporting on or marking and tracing of ammunition or explosives [and] there will be no mandate for an international body to enforce an ATT."[10]

An Alternative Security System requires a major level of disarmament in order for all nations to feel safe from aggression. The UN defines general and complete disarmament "…as the elimination of all WMD, coupled with the "balanced reduction of armed forces and conventional armaments, based on the principle of undiminished security of the parties with a view to promoting or enhancing stability at a lower military level, taking into account the need of all States to protect their security" (UN General Assembly, Final Document of the First Special Session on Disarmament, para. 22.) This definition of disarmament seems to have holes large enough to drive a tank through. A much more aggressive treaty with dated reduction levels is required, as well as an enforcement mechanism.

The Treaty appears to do no more than require States Parties to create an agency to oversee arms exports and imports and to determine if they think the arms will be misused for such activities as genocide or piracy and to report annually on their trade. It does not appear to do the job since it leaves the control of the trade up to those who want to export and import. A far more vigorous and enforceable ban on the export of arms is necessary. The arms trade needs to be added to the International Criminal Court's list of "crimes against humanity" and enforced in the case of individual arms manufacturers and traders and by the Security Council in its mandate to confront violations of "international peace and security" in the case of sovereign states as the selling agents.[11]

---

9. For comprehensive information and data see the website of the Organization for the Prohibition of Chemical Weapons (https://www.opcw.org/), which received the 2013 Nobel Peace Prize for its extensive efforts to eliminate chemical weapons.

10. See the U.S. State Departments Arms Trade Treaty documentation at: http://www.state.gov/t/isn/armstradetreaty/

11. Estimates range from 600,000 (Battle Deaths Dataset) to 1,250,000 (Correlates of War Project). It should be noted, that measuring casualties of war is a controversial topic. Importantly, indirect war-deaths are not accurately measurable. Indirect casualties can be traced back to the following: destruction of infrastructure; landmines; use of depleted uranium; refugees and internally displaced people; malnutrition; diseases;

End the Use of Militarized Drones

Drones are pilotless aircraft (as well as submarines and other robots) maneuvered remotely from a distance of thousands of miles. Thus far, the main deployer of military drones has been the United States. "Predator" and "Reaper" drones carry rocket-propelled high explosive warheads which can be targeted on people. They are maneuvered by "pilots" sitting at computer terminals in Nevada and elsewhere. These drones are regularly used for so-called targeted killings against people in Pakistan, Yemen, Afghanistan, Somalia, Iraq, and Syria. The justification for these attacks, which have killed hundreds of civilians, is the highly questionable doctrine of "anticipatory defense." The U.S. President has determined that he can, with the aid of a special panel, order the death of anyone deemed to be a terrorist threat to the U.S., even U.S. citizens for whom the Constitution requires due process of law, conveniently ignored in this case. In fact, the U.S. Constitution requires respect of everyone's rights, not making the distinction for U.S. citizens that we are taught. And among the targeted are people never identified but deemed suspicious by their behavior, a parallel to racial profiling by domestic police.

The problems with drone attacks are legal, moral, and practical. First, they are a clear violation of every nation's laws against murder and of U.S. law under executive orders issued against assassinations by the U.S. government as far back as 1976 by President Gerald Ford and later reiterated by President Ronald Reagan. Used against U.S. citizens – or anyone else – these killings violate the rights of due process under the U.S. Constitution. And while current international law under Article 51 of the UN Charter legalizes self-defense in the case of an armed attack, drones nevertheless appear to violate international law as well as the Geneva Conventions.[12] While drones might be considered legally used in a combat zone in a declared war, the U.S. has not declared war in all of the countries where it kills with drones, nor are any of its current wars legal under the UN Charter or the Kellogg-Briand Pact, nor is it clear what makes certain wars "declared" as the U.S. Congress has not declared war since 1941.

Further, the doctrine of anticipatory defense, which states that a nation can legitimately use force when it anticipates it might be attacked, is questioned by many international law experts. The problem with such an interpretation of international law is its ambiguity—how does a nation know for certain that what another state or non-state actor says and does would truly lead to an armed attack? In fact, any would-be aggressor could actually hide behind this doctrine to justify its aggression. At the least, it could be (and is presently) used indiscriminately without oversight by Congress or the United Nations.

Second, drone attacks are clearly immoral even under the conditions of "just war doctrine" which stipulates that non-combatants are not to be attacked in warfare. Many of the drone attacks are not targeted on known individuals whom the government designates as terrorists, but simply against gatherings where such people are suspected to be present. Many civilians have been killed in these attacks and there is evidence that on some occasions, when rescuers have gathered at the site after the first attack, a second strike has been ordered to kill the rescuers. Many of the dead have been children.[13]

2016 Developments:

The U.S. government released a long-anticipated account acknowledging the death toll of U.S. drone strikes. Not surprisingly, the released civilian and combatant - a distinction drone warfare blurries - death toll is far lower than any other credible estimates show.

---

lawlessness; intra-state killings; victims of rape and other forms of sexual violence; social injustice. Read more at: The human costs of war – definitional and methodological ambiguity of casualties (http://bit.ly/victimsofwar)

12. See Geneva Convention Rule 14. Proportionality in Attack (https://ihl-databases.icrc.org/customary-ihl/eng/docs/v1_cha_chapter4_rule14)

13. The comprehensive report Living Under Drones. Death, Injury and Trauma to Civilians from U.S. Drone Practices in Pakistan (2012) by the Stanford International Human Rights and Conflict Resolution Clinic and the Global Justice Clinic at NYU School of Law demonstrates that the U.S. narratives of "targeted killings" is false. The report shows that civilians are injured and killed, drone strikes cause considerable harm to the daily lives of civilians, the evidence that strikes have made the U.S. safer is ambiguous at best, and that drone strike

Third, drone attacks are counter-productive. While purporting to kill enemies of the U.S. (a sometimes dubious claim), they create intense resentment for the U.S. and are easily used in recruiting new terrorists.

> *For every innocent person you kill, you create ten new enemies.*

General Stanley McChrystal (former Commander, U.S. and NATO Forces in Afghanistan)

Further, by arguing that its drone attacks are legal even when war has not been declared, the U.S provides justification for other nations or groups to claim legality when they may well want to use drones to attack the U.S. Drone attacks make a nation that uses them less rather than more secure.

> *When you drop a bomb from a drone… you are going to cause more damage than you are going to cause good,*

U.S. Lt. General Michael Flynn (ret.)

More than seventy nations now possess drones, and more than 50 countries are developing them.[14] The rapid development of the technology and production capacity suggest that almost every nation will be able to have armed drones within a decade. Some War System advocates have said that the defense against drone attacks will be to build drones that attack drones, demonstrating the way in which War System thinking typically leads to arms races and greater instability while widening the destruction when a particular war breaks out. Outlawing militarized drones by any and all nations and groups would be a major step forward in demilitarizing security.

> *Drones are not named Predators and Reapers for nothing. They are killing machines. With no judge or jury, they obliterate lives in an instant, the lives of those deemed by someone, somewhere, to be terrorists, along with those who are accidentally—or incidentally—caught in their cross-hairs.*

Medea Benjamin (Activist, Author, Co-founder of CODEPINK)

Phase Out Weapons Of Mass Destruction

Weapons of mass destruction are a powerful positive feedback to the War System, strengthening its spread and ensuring that wars that do occur have the potential for planet-altering destruction. Nuclear, chemical and biological weapons are characterized by their ability to kill and maim enormous numbers of people, wiping out whole cities and even whole regions with indescribable destruction.

Nuclear Weapons

At present there are treaties banning biological and chemical weapons but there is no treaty banning nuclear weapons. The 1970 Non-Proliferation Treaty (NPT) provides that five recognized nuclear weapons states– the U.S., Russia, UK, France and China– should make good faith efforts for the elimination of nuclear weapons, while all other

---

practices are undermine international law. The full report can be read here: http://www.livingunderdrones.org/wp-content/uploads/2013/10/Stanford-NYU-Living-Under-Drones.pdf

14. See the report Armed and Dangerous. UAVs and U.S. Security by the Rand Corporation at: http://www.rand.org/content/dam/rand/pubs/research_reports/RR400/RR449/RAND_RR449.pdf

NPT signatories pledge not to acquire nuclear weapons. Only three countries refused to join the NPT— India, Pakistan, and Israel—and they acquired nuclear arsenals. North Korea, relying on the NPT bargain for "peaceful" nuclear technology, walked out of the treaty using its "peaceful" technology to develop fissile materials for nuclear power to manufacture nuclear bombs.[15] Indeed, every nuclear power plant is a potential bomb factory.

A war fought with even a so-called "limited" number of nuclear weapons would kill millions, induce nuclear winter and result in worldwide food shortages that would result in the starvation of millions. The whole nuclear strategy system rests upon a false foundation, because computer models suggest that only a very small percentage of warheads detonated could cause the worldwide shutdown of agriculture for up to a decade—in effect, a death sentence for the human species. And the trend at present is toward a greater and greater likelihood of some systemic failure of equipment or communication that would lead to nuclear weapons being used.

A larger release could extinguish all life on the planet. These weapons threaten the security of everyone everywhere.[16] While various nuclear arms control treaties between the U.S. and the former Soviet Union did reduce the insane number of nuclear weapons (56,000 at one point), there are still 16,300 in the world, only 1000 of which are not in the U.S. or Russia.[17] What is worse, the treaties allowed for "modernization," a euphemism for creating a new generation of weapons and delivery systems, which all of the nuclear states are doing. The nuclear monster has not gone away; it is not even lurking in the back of the cave—it's out in the open and costing billions of dollars that could be far better used elsewhere. Since the not so Comprehensive Test Ban Treaty was signed in 1998, the U.S. has ramped up its high-tech laboratory tests of nuclear weapons, coupled with sub-critical tests, 1,000 feet below the desert floor at the Nevada test site on Western Shoshone land. The U.S. has performed 28 such tests to date, blowing up plutonium with chemicals, without causing a chain-reaction, hence "sub-critical".[18] Indeed, the Obama administration is currently projecting expenditures of one trillion dollars over the next thirty years for new bomb factories and delivery systems—missiles, airplanes submarines—as well as new nuclear weapons.[19]

Conventional War System thinking argues that nuclear weapons deter war–the so-called doctrine of "Mutual Assured Destruction" ("MAD"). While it is true that they have not been used since 1945, it is not logical to conclude that MAD has been the reason. As Daniel Ellsberg has pointed out, every U.S. president since Truman has used nuclear weapons as a threat to other nations to get them to allow the U.S. to get its way. Furthermore, such a doctrine rests on a wobbly faith in the rationality of political leaders in a crisis situation, for all time to come. MAD does not ensure security against either accidental release of these monstrous weapons or a strike by a nation that mistakenly thought it was under attack or a pre-emptive first strike. In fact, certain kinds of nuclear warhead delivery systems have been designed and built for the latter purpose— the Cruise Missile (which sneaks under radar) and the Pershing Missile, a fast attack, forward-based missile. Serious discussions actually occurred during the Cold War about the desirability of a "Grand, Decapitating First Strike" in which the U.S. would initiate a nuclear attack on the Soviet Union in order to disable its ability to launch nuclear weapons by obliterating command and control, beginning with the Kremlin. Some analysts wrote about "winning" a nuclear war in which only a few tens of millions would be killed, nearly all civilians.[20] Nuclear weapons are patently immoral and insane.

15. http://en.wikipedia.org/wiki/Treaty_on_the_Non-Proliferation_of_Nuclear_Weapons

16. See the report by Nobel Peace Laureate Organization International Physicians for the Prevention of Nuclear War "Nuclear Famine: two billion people at risk"

17. ibid

18. ibid

19. http://nnsa.energy.gov/mediaroom/pressreleases/pollux120612

20. http://www.nytimes.com/2014/09/22/us/us-ramping-up-major-renewal-in-nuclear-arms.html?_r=0

2016 Development:

The so-called Iran Nuclear Deal is considered a success as a viable alternative to war. The deal's objective is to prevent Iran from developing a nuclear weapon and lifting nuclear sanctions imposed on the nation. Nevertheless, there is continued debate and pressure from right wing political forces, who consider the deal weak and dangerous. Peace scholar David Cortright reminds us not only to celebrate occasions where diplomacy prevailed, but understand and defend the processes, so that diplomacy can be applied again in other settings.

Even if they are not used deliberately, there have been numerous incidents where nuclear weapons carried in airplanes have crashed to the ground, fortunately only spewing some plutonium on the ground, but not going off.[21] In 2007, six U.S. missiles carrying nuclear warheads were mistakenly flown from North Dakota to Louisiana and the missing nuclear bombs were not discovered for 36 hours.[22] There have been reports of drunkenness and poor performance by servicemen posted in underground silos responsible for launching U.S. nuclear missiles poised on hair-trigger alert and pointed at Russian cities.[23] The U.S. and Russia each have thousands of nuclear missiles primed and ready to be fired at each other. A Norwegian weather satellite went off-course over Russia and was almost taken for an incoming attack until the last minute when utter chaos was averted.[24]

History does not make us, we make it—or end it.

Thomas Merton (Catholic Writer)

The 1970 NPT was due to expire in 1995, and it was extended indefinitely at that time, with a provision for five year review conferences and preparatory meetings in between. To gain consensus for the NPT extension, the governments promised to hold a conference to negotiate a Weapons of Mass Destruction Free Zone in the Middle East. At each of the five year review conferences, new promises were given, such as for an unequivocal commitment to the total elimination of nuclear weapons, and for various "steps" that need to be taken for a nuclear free world, none of which have been honored.[25] A Model Nuclear Weapons Convention, drafted by civil society with scientists, lawyers, and other experts was adopted by the UN[26] which provided, "all States would be prohibited from pursuing or participating in the 'development, testing, production, stockpiling, transfer, use and threat of use of nuclear weapons.'" It provided for all the steps that would be needed to destroy arsenals and guard materials under verified international control.[27]

To the dismay of civil society and many non-nuclear weapons states, none of the proposed steps at the many NPT review conferences have been adopted. Following an important initiative by the International Red Cross to make known the catastrophic humanitarian consequences of nuclear weapons, a new campaign to negotiate a simple ban treaty without the participation of the nuclear weapons states was launched in Oslo in 2013, with follow up conferences in Nayarit, Mexico and Vienna in 2014.[28]

21. http://www.strategicstudiesinstitute.army.mil/pdffiles/pub585.pdf

22. http://en.wikipedia.org/wiki/List_of_military_nuclear_accidents

23. http://en.wikipedia.org/wiki/2007_United_States_Air_Force_nuclear_weapons_incident

24. http://cdn.defenseone.com/defenseone/interstitial.html?v=2.1.1&rf=http%3A%2F%2Fwww.defenseone.com%2Fideas%2F2014%2F11%2Flast-thing-us-needs-are-mobile-nuclear-missiles%2F98828%2F

25. See also, Eric Schlosser, Command and Control: Nuclear Weapons, the Damascus Accident, and the Illusion of Safety; http://en.wikipedia.org/wiki/Stanislav_Petrov

26. http://www.armscontrol.org/act/2005_04/LookingBack

27. http://www.inesap.org/book/securing-our-survival

28. Those States that possess nuclear weapons would be obligated to destroy their nuclear arsenals in a series of phases. These five phases would progress as follows: taking nuclear weapons off alert, removing weapons from deployment, removing nuclear warheads from their delivery vehicles, disabling the warheads, removing and disfiguring the 'pits' and placing the fissile material under international control. Under the model convention, delivery vehicles would also have to be destroyed or converted to a non-nuclear capability. In addition, the NWC would prohibit the production of weapons-usable fissile material. The States Parties would also establish an Agency for the Prohibition of Nuclear Weapons that would be tasked with verification, ensuring compliance, decision-making, and providing a forum for consultation and cooperation among all State Parties. The Agency would be comprised of a Conference of State Parties, an Executive Council and a Technical Secretariat. Declarations would be required from all States Parties regarding all nuclear weapons, material, facilities, and delivery vehicles in their possession or control along with their locations." Compliance: Under the 2007 model

There is momentum to open these negotiations after the 2015 NPT Review conference, on the 70th Anniversary of the terrible destruction of Hiroshima and Nagasaki. At the Vienna meeting, the government of Austria announced a pledge to work for a nuclear weapons ban, described as "taking effective measures to fill the legal gap for the prohibition and elimination of nuclear weapons" and "to cooperate with all stakeholders to achieve this goal."[29] Additionally, the Vatican spoke out at this conference and for the first time declared that nuclear deterrence is immoral and the weapons should be banned.[30] A ban treaty will put pressure not only on the nuclear weapons states, but on the governments sheltering under the U.S. nuclear umbrella, in NATO countries which rely on nuclear weapons for "deterrence" as well as countries like Australia, Japan and South Korea.[31] Additionally, the U.S. stations about 400 nuclear bombs in NATO states, Belgium, the Netherlands, Italy, Germany and Turkey, who will also be pressured to give up their "nuclear sharing arrangements" and sign the ban treaty.[32][33]

Chemical and Biological Weapons

Biological weapons consist of deadly natural toxins such as Ebola, typhus, smallpox, and others that have been altered in the lab to be super virulent so there is no antidote. Their use could start an uncontrolled global epidemic. Therefore it is critical to adhere to existing treaties that already make up part of an Alternative Security System. The Convention on the Prohibition of the Development, Production and Stockpiling of Bacteriological (Biological) and Toxin Weapons and on their Destruction was opened for signature in 1972 and went into force in 1975 under the aegis of the United Nations. It prohibits the 170 signatories from possessing or developing or stockpiling these weapons. However, it lacks a verification mechanism and needs to be strengthened by a rigorous challenge inspection regime (i.e., any State can challenge another which has agreed in advance to an inspection.)

The Convention on the Prohibition of the Development, Production, Stockpiling and Use of Chemical Weapons and on their Destruction prohibits the development, production, acquisition, stockpiling, retention, transfer or use of chemical weapons. States Signatories have agreed to destroy any stockpiles of chemical weapons they may hold and any facilities which produced them, as well as any chemical weapons they abandoned on the territory of other States in the past and to create a challenge verification regime for certain toxic chemicals and their precursors… in order to ensure that such chemicals are only used for purposes not prohibited. The convention entered into force on April 29, 1997. Whereas the world stockpiles of chemical weapons have been dramatically reduced, complete destruction is still a distant goal.[34] The treaty was

NWC, "States Parties would be required to adopt legislative measures to provide for the prosecution of persons committing crimes and protection for persons reporting violations of the Convention. States would also be required to establish a national authority responsible for national tasks in implementation. The Convention would apply rights and obligations not only to the States Parties but also to individuals and legal entities. Legal disputes over the Convention could be referred to the ICJ [International Court of Justice] with mutual consent of States Parties. The Agency would also have the ability to request an advisory opinion from the ICJ over a legal dispute. The Convention would also provide for a series of graduated responses to evidence of non-compliance beginning with consultation, clarification, and negotiation. If necessary, cases could be referred to the UN General Assembly and Security Council." [Source: Nuclear Threat Initiative, http://www.nti.org/treaties-and-regimes/proposed-nuclear-weapons-convention-nwc/]

29. www.icanw.org

30. https://www.opendemocracy.net/5050/rebecca-johnson/austrian-pledge-to-ban-nuclear-weapons

31. http://www.paxchristi.net/sites/default/files/nuclearweaponstimeforabolitionfinal.pdf

32. https://www.armscontrol.org/act/2012_06/NATO_Sticks_With_Nuclear_Policy

33. A citizen initiative by PAX in the Netherlands calls for a ban of nuclear weapons in the Netherlands. Read the proposal at: http://www.paxforpeace.nl/media/files/pax-proposal-citizens-initiatiative-2016-eng.pdf

34. http://en.wikipedia.org/wiki/Nuclear_sharing

successfully implemented in 2014, when Syria turned over its stockpiles of chemical weapons. The decision to pursue that result was made by U.S. President Barack Obama shortly after he reversed his decision to launch a major bombing campaign over Syria, the nonviolent disarmament measure serving as something of a public substitute for a war measure prevented largely by public pressure.

Outlaw Weapons In Outer Space

Several countries have developed plans and even hardware for warfare in outer space including ground to space and space to space weapons to attack satellites, and space to ground weapons (including laser weapons) to attack earth installations from space. The dangers of placing weapons in outer space are obvious, especially in the case of nuclear weapons or advanced technology weapons. 130 nations now have space programs and there are 3000 operational satellites in space. The dangers include undermining existing weapons conventions and starting a new arms race. If such a space-based war were to occur the consequences would be terrifying for earth's inhabitants as well as risking the dangers of the Kessler Syndrome, a scenario in which the density of objects in low earth orbit is high enough that attacking some would start a cascade of collisions generating enough space debris to render space exploration or even the use of satellites infeasible for decades, possibly generations.

Believing it had the lead in this type of weapons R&D, "Assistant Secretary of the United States Air Force for Space, Keith R. Hall, said, 'With regard to space dominance, we have it, we like it and we're going to keep it.'"

The 1967 Outer Space Treaty was reaffirmed in 1999 by 138 nations with only the U.S. and Israel abstaining. It prohibits WMDs in space and the construction of military bases on the moon but leaves a loophole for conventional, laser and high energy particle beam weapons. The United Nations Committee on Disarmament has struggled for years to get consensus on a treaty banning these weapons but has been continually blocked by the United States. A weak, non-binding, voluntary Code of Conduct has been proposed but "the U.S. is insisting on a provision in this third version of the Code of Conduct that, while making a voluntary promise to 'refrain from any action which brings about, directly or indirectly, damage, or destruction, of space objects', qualifies that directive with the language "unless such action is justified". "Justification" is based on the right of self-defense that is built into the UN Charter. Such a qualification renders even a voluntary agreement meaningless. A more robust treaty banning all weapons in outer space is a necessary component of an Alternative Security System.[35]

End Invasions and Occupations

The occupation of one people by another is a major threat to security and peace, resulting in structural violence that often promotes the occupied to mount various levels of attacks from "terrorist" assaults to guerrilla warfare. Prominent examples are: Israel's occupation of the West Bank and assaults on Gaza, and China's occupation of Tibet. Even the strong U.S. military presence in Germany, and even more so Japan, some 70 years after World War II has not prompted a violent response, but does create resentment, as do U.S. troops in many of the 175 nations where they are now based.

Even when the invading and occupying power has overwhelming military capability, these adventures usually do not work out due to several factors. First, they are

Photo: U.S. Navy photo by Photographer's Mate 2nd Class Michael D. Heckman [Public domain], via Wikimedia Commons

35. A draft sample treaty to achieve this can be seen at the Global Network for the Prohibition of Weapons and Nuclear Power In Space, at http://www.space4peace.org

Article 7 of the Rome Statute of the International Criminal Court identifies the crimes against humanity.

enormously expensive. Second, they are often pitted against those who have a greater stake in the conflict because they are fighting to protect their homeland. Third, even "victories," as in Iraq, are elusive and leave the countries devastated and politically fractured. Fourth, once in, it's hard to get out, as the U.S. invasion of Afghanistan exemplifies which officially "ended" in December, 2014 after thirteen years, although almost 10,000 U.S. troops remain in country. Finally, and foremost, invasions and armed occupations against resistance kill more civilians than resistance fighters and create millions of refugees.

Invasions are outlawed by the UN Charter, unless they are in retaliation for a prior invasion, an inadequate provision. The presence of troops of one country inside another with or without an invitation destabilizes global security and makes conflicts more likely to be militarized and would be prohibited in an Alternative Security System.

Realign Military Spending, Convert Infrastructure to Produce Funding For Civilian Needs (Economic Conversion)

Demilitarizing security as described above will eliminate the need for many weapons programs and military bases, providing an opportunity for government and military-dependent corporations to switch these resources to creating genuine wealth. It can also reduce the tax burden on society and create more jobs. In the U.S., for every $1 billion spent in the military more than twice the number of jobs at wider spectrum of pay grades would be created if the same amount were spent in the civilian sector.[36] The trade-offs from shifting federal spending priorities with U.S. tax dollars away from the military toward other programs are tremendous.[37]

Spending on a militarized national "defense" is astronomical. The United States alone spends more than the next 15 countries combined on its military.[38]

The United States spends $1.3 trillion dollars annually on the Pentagon Budget, nuclear weapons (in the Energy Department budget), veteran's services, the CIA and Homeland Security.[39] The world as a whole spends over $2 trillion. Numbers of this magnitude are hard to grasp. Note that 1 million seconds equals 12 days, 1 billion seconds equals 32 years, and 1 trillion seconds equals 32,000 years. And yet, the highest level of military spending in the world was unable to prevent the 9/11 attacks, halt nuclear proliferation, end terrorism, or suppress resistance to occupations in the Middle East. No matter how much money is spent on war, it does not work.

Military spending is also a serious drain on a nation's economic strength, as pioneering economist Adam Smith pointed out. Smith argued that military spending was economically unproductive. Decades ago, economists commonly used "military burden" almost synonymously with "military budget." Currently, military industries in the U.S. receive more capital from the state than all private industries combined can command. Transferring this investment capital to the free market sector either directly by grants for conversion or by lowering taxes or paying down the national debt (with its huge annual interest payments) would inject a huge incentive for economic development.

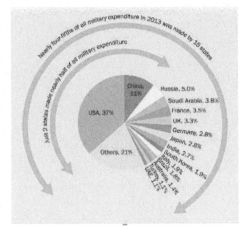

Graphic: The share of world military expenditure of the 15 states with the highest expenditure in 2013 (Source: Trends in World Military Expenditure by Stockholm International Peace Research Institute)

---

36. Researchers found that investments in clean energy, healthcare and education create a much larger number of jobs across all pay ranges than spending the same amount of funds with the military. For the complete study see: *The U.S. Employment Effects of Military and Domestic Spending Priorities: 2011 Update* at http://www.peri.umass.edu/fileadmin/pdf/published_study/PERI_military_spending_2011.pdf

37. Try the National Priorities Projects's Trade -Offs calculator to see what U.S. tax dollars could have paid for instead of 2015 Department of Defense budget: https://www.nationalpriorities.org/interactive-data/trade-offs/

38. See the Stockholm International Peace Research Institute Military Expenditure Database.

39. Download the War Resisters League federal spending pie chart at https://www.warresisters.org/sites/default/files/2015%20pie%20chart%20-%20high%20res.pdf

A Security System combining the elements described above (and to be described in following sections) would cost a fraction of the present U.S. military budget and would underwrite a process of economic conversion. Furthermore, it would create more jobs. One billion dollars of federal investment in the military creates 11,200 jobs whereas the same investment in clean energy technology would yield 16,800, in health care 17,200 and in education 26,700.[40]

Economic conversion requires changes in technology, economics and the political process for shifting from military to civilian markets. It is the process of transferring the human and material resources used to make one product to the making of a different one; for example, converting from building missiles to building light rail cars. It is not a mystery: private industry does it all the time. Converting the military industry to making products of use value to society would add to the economic strength of a nation instead of detracting from it. Resources presently employed in making weapons and maintaining military bases could be redirected to many areas of domestic investment and foreign aid. Infrastructure is always in need of repair and upgrading including transportation infrastructure such as roads, bridges, and rail network, as well as energy grids, schools, water and sewer systems, and renewable energy installations, etc. Just imagine Flint, Michigan and the many other cities where citizens, mostly poor minorities, are poisoned with lead-contaminated water. Another investment area is innovation leading to reindustrialization of economies that are overloaded with low-paying service industries and far too dependent on debt payments and foreign imports of goods, a practice that also adds to the carbon loading of the atmosphere. Airbases, for example, can be converted to shopping malls and housing developments or entrepreneurship incubators or solar-panel arrays.

The main obstacles to economic conversion, apart from the corruption of government by money, are the fear of job loss and the need to retrain both labor and management. Jobs will need to be guaranteed by the state while the retraining takes place, or other forms of compensation paid to those currently working in the military industry in order to avoid a negative impact on the economy of major unemployment during the transition from a war to a peacetime status.

To be successful, conversion needs to be part of a larger political program of arms reduction. It will require national level meta-planning and financial assistance and intensive local planning as communities with military bases envision transformation and corporations determine what their new niche can be in the free market. This will require tax dollars but in the end will save far more than is invested in redevelopment as states end the economic drain of military spending and replace it with profitable peace time economies creating useful consumer goods.

Attempts have been made to legislate conversion, such as the Nuclear Disarmament and Economic Conversion Act of 1999, which links nuclear disarmament to conversion.

> *The bill would require the United States to disable and dismantle its nuclear weapons and to refrain from replacing them with weapons of mass destruction once foreign countries possessing nuclear weapons enact and execute similar requirements. The bill also provides that the resources used to sustain our nuclear weapons program be used to address human and infrastructure needs such as housing, health care, education, agriculture, and the environment. So I would see a direct transfer of funds.*

(Transcript of July 30, 1999, Press Conference) HR-2545: "Nuclear Disarmament and Economic Conversion Act of 1999"

---

40. See: The U.S. Employment Effects of Military and Domestic Spending Priorities: 2011 Update at http://www.peri.umass.edu/fileadmin/pdf/published_study/PERI_military_spending_2011.pdf

Legislation of this sort requires more public support to pass. Success may grow from a smaller scale. The state of Connecticut has created a commission to work on transition. Other states and localities may follow Connecticut's lead. Some momentum for this grew out of a misperception that military spending was being reduced in Washington. We need to either prolong that misperception, make it a reality (obviously the best choice), or persuade local and state governments to take the initiative anyway.

Reconfigure The Response to Terrorism

Following the 9/11 attacks on the World Trade Center, the U.S. attacked terrorist bases in Afghanistan, initiating a long, unsuccessful war. Adopting a military approach has not only failed to end terrorism, it has resulted in the erosion of constitutional liberties, the commission of human rights abuses and violations of international law, and has provided cover for dictators and democratic governments to further abuse their powers, justifying abuses in the name of "fighting terrorism."

The terrorist threat to people in the Western world has been exaggerated and there has been an over-reaction in the media, public and political realm. Many benefit from exploiting the threat of terrorism in what now can be called a homeland-security-industrial complex. As Glenn Greenwald writes:

> *...the private and public entities that shape government policy and drive political discourse profit far too much in numerous ways to allow rational considerations of the Terror threat.[41]*

One of the end results of the over-reaction to the terrorist threat has been a proliferation of violent and hostile extremists such as ISIS.[42] In this particular case, there are many constructive nonviolent alternatives to counter ISIS which should not be mistaken for inaction. These include: an arms embargo, support of Syrian civil society, support of nonviolent civil resistance,[43] pursuit of meaningful diplomacy with all actors, economic sanctions on ISIS and supporters, closing the border to cut off the sale of oil from ISIS controlled territories and stop the flow of fighters, and humanitarian aid. Long-term strong steps would be the withdrawal of U.S. troops from the region and ending oil imports from the region in order to dissolve terrorism at its roots.[44]

In general, a more effective strategy than war would be to treat terrorist attacks as crimes against humanity instead of acts of war, and to use all the resources of the international police community to bring perpetrators to justice before the International Criminal Court. It is notable that an incredibly powerful military was unable to prevent the worst attacks on the U.S. since Pearl Harbor.

> *The world's most powerful military did nothing to prevent or stop the 9-11 attacks. Virtually every terrorist caught, every terrorist plot foiled has been the result of first-rate intelligence and police work, not the threat*

41. The following are only some of the analyses dealing with the exaggerated terrorism threats: Lisa Stampnitzky's *Disciplining Terror. How Experts Invented 'Terrorism'*; Stephen Walt's *What terrorist threat?*; John Mueller and Mark Stewart's *The Terrorism Delusion. America's Overwrought Response to September 11*

42. See Glenn Greenwald, The sham "terrorism" expert industry at http://www.salon.com/2012/08/15/the_sham_terrorism_expert_industry/

43. See Maria Stephan, Defeating ISIS Through Civil Resistance? Striking Nonviolently at Sources of Power Could Support Effective Solutions at http://www.usip.org/olivebranch/2016/07/11/defeating-isis-through-civil-resistance

44. Comprehensive discussions outlining viable, nonviolent alternatives to the ISIS threat can be found at http://worldbeyondwar.org/new-war-forever-war-world-beyond-war/ and http://warpreventioninitiative.org/images/PDF/ISIS_matrix_report.pdf

Some key findings of the 2015 Global Terrorism Index: Terrorism in 2014 reached the highest level ever. 88% of all terrorist attacks since 1989 occurred in countries that experienced or were involved in violent conflict. Only 0.5% of terrorist attacks have occurred in the West since 2000. The U.S. invasion of Iraq and the Syrian civil war led to an increase in terrorism.

or use of military force. Military force has also been useless in preventing the spread of weapons of mass destruction.

Lloyd J. Dumas (Professor of Political Economy)

A professional field of peace and conflict studies scholars and practitioners is continuously providing responses to terrorism which are superior to the so-called experts of the terrorism industry.

> BUT WHAT ABOUT THE CASES WHEN INNOCENTS ARE FACING ATROCITIES? WE HAVE TO DO SOMETHING, RIGHT?

> ABSOLUTELY. LET'S JUST NOT THINK THAT THE ONLY CHOICES WE HAVE ARE EITHER A MILITARY INTERVENTION OR INACTION.

NONVIOLENT RESPONSES TO TERRORISM

- Arms embargoes
- End all military aid
- Civil Society Support, Nonviolent actors
- Sanctions
- Work through supranational bodies (e.g. UN, ICC)
- Ceasefires
- Aid to refugees (relocate/improve proximal camps/repatriate)
- Pledge no use of violence
- Withdrawal of military
- Nonviolent conflict workers
- (Transitional) Justice Initiatives
- Meaningful diplomacy
- Conflict resolution framework
- Inclusive good governance
- Confront violence supporting beliefs
- Increasing women's participation in social and political life
- Accurate information on facts
- Separate perpetrators from support base – addressing the grey area

- Ban war profiteering
- Peacebuilding engagement; reframe the either/or us/them choices
- Effective policing
- Nonviolent Civil Resistance
- Information gathering and reporting
- Public advocacy
- Conciliation, arbitration and judicial settlement
- Human rights mechanisms
- Humanitarian assistance and protection
- Economic, political and strategic inducements
- Monitoring, observation and verification

LONG-TERM NONVIOLENT RESPONSES TO TERRORISM[45]

- Stop and reverse all arms trade and manufacture
- Consumption reduction by rich nations
- Massive aid to poor nations and populations
- Refugee repatriation or emigration
- Debt relief to poorest nations
- Education about roots of terrorism
- Education and training about nonviolent power
- Promote culturally and ecologically sensitive tourism and cultural exchanges
- Build sustainable and just economy, energy use and distribution, agriculture

> IF WE DON'T USE THESE ALTERNATIVES, IT IS NOT BECAUSE THEY ARE UNAVAILABLE, BUT BECAUSE OF ARTIFICIALLY IMPOSED CONSTRAINTS, LACK OF INTEREST, OR SELF-INTEREST. WHILE THESE SOLUTIONS ARE NOT MAGICAL, THEY DO WORK. WE HAVE TO LOOK AT THEM IN TERMS OF EFFECTIVENESS VERSUS THE MILITARY INTERVENTION. AND IT IS BEYOND DOUBT THAT THEY ARE MORE EFFECTIVE AS SHORT-, MEDIUM-, AND LONG-TERM RESPONSES.

Dismantle Military Alliances

Military alliances such as the North Atlantic Treaty Organization (NATO) are leftovers from the Cold War. With the collapse of the Soviet client states in Eastern Europe, the Warsaw Pact alliance disappeared, but NATO expanded up to the borders of the former Soviet Union in violation of a promise to former premier Gorbachev, and has resulted in extreme tension between Russia and the West— the beginnings of a new Cold War–signaled perhaps by a U.S. supported coup in Ukraine, the Russian annexation of, or reunification with the Crimea - depending on which narrative prevails - and the civil war in Ukraine. This new cold war could too easily become a nuclear war which could kill hundreds of millions of people. NATO is a positive reinforcement of the War System, reducing rather than creating security. NATO has also taken on military exercises well beyond the borders of Europe. It has become a force for militarized efforts in eastern Europe, North Africa and the Middle East.

---

45. All responses are thoroughly examined in: Hastings, Tom H. 2004. *Nonviolent Response to Terrorism.*

> Giving representatives from the entire community a voice in peace and reconciliation processes after an armed conflict, is essential for achieving long-term peace. In most cases, however, half of the population is routinely excluded from this process.
>
> (More women in peace processes at
>
> http://kvinnatillkvinna.se/en/what-we-do/
>
> more-women-in-peace-processes/)

> When women are excluded from peace processes, the experiences, knowledge and needs of half of the population are lost before the country's efforts to rebuild have even begun.
>
> (More women in peace processes at
>
> http://kvinnatillkvinna.se/en/what-we-do/
>
> more-women-in-peace-processes/)

The Role of Women in Peace and Security

The role of women in peace and security has not been given the appropriate attention. Take for example treaties, in particular peace agreements, which are most commonly negotiated and signed in a male dominated context, by state and non-state armed actors. This context utterly misses the reality on the ground. The "Better Peace Tool" by the International Civil Society Action Network was developed as a guide to inclusive peace processes and negotiations.[46] Women, according to the report, share a vision of societies rooted in social justice and equality, are an important source of practical experience about life in a war zone, and understand the ground realities (e.g. radicalization and peacemaking). Peace processes therefore should not be narrowly focused security or political ones, but inclusive societal processes. This is what is called the democratization of peacemaking.

"No women, no peace" - this headline described the central role of women and gender equality in the peace deal between the Colombian government and the FARC rebel group, marking the end of a 50-plus-year civil war in August of 2016. The deal does not only have women influence on the content, but also on the manner in which peace is built. A gender subcommission ensures lines by line that women's perspectives are ensured, even LGBT rights are considered.[47]

There are numerous examples of creative and determined women peace activists in the secular and faith-based realms. Sister Joan Chittister has been a leading voice for women, peace and justice for decades. Iranian Nobel Peace Prize Laureate Shirin Ebadi is an outspoken advocate against nuclear weapons. Worldwide indigenous women are increasingly recognized and powerful as agents of social change. A less known, but nonetheless wonderful example is the Young Women's Peace Charter aimed at building commitment and understanding of the challenges and obstacles faced by young women in conflict affected countries, as well as other societies within the framework of the Young Women's Peace Academy.[48] The women want to spread feminism worldwide, eliminate patriarchal structures, and secure the safety for feminists, women peacebuilders and human rights defenders. The goals are accompanied by a powerful set of recommendations which can act as a model for women in many contexts.

Women played a particular role in peace talks in Guatemala in the 1990s, they formed an alliance to coordinate peacebuilding activity in Somalia, they forge cross-community efforts in the Israeli-Palestinian conflict, or led a political movement to enhances women's power and influence the peace agreement and peace processes in Northern Ireland.[49] Women's voices advance different agendas from the those usually presented by leaders.[50]

Acknowledging the existing gap in the role of women and peacebuilding, advances have been made. Most notably at the policy level, UNSCR 1325 (2000) provides a "global framework for mainstreaming gender in all peace processes, including peacekeeping, peacebuilding, and postconflict reconstruction."[51] At the same time, it is clear that policies and rhetorical commitments are only a first step toward changing a male-dominated paradigm.

46. http://www.betterpeacetool.org

47. No women, no peace. Colombian women made sure gender equality was at the center of a groundbreaking peace deal with the FARC (http://qz.com/768092/colombian-women-made-sure-gender-equality-was-at-the-center-of-a-groundbreaking-peace-deal-with-the-farc/)

48. http://kvinnatillkvinna.se/en/files/qbank/6f221fcb5c504fe96789df252123770b.pdf

49. Ramsbotham, Oliver, Hugh Miall, and Tom Woodhouse. 2016. *Contemporary Conflict Resolution: The Prevention, Management and Transformation of Deadly Conflicts*. 4thed. Cambridge: Polity.

50. See "Women, Religion, and Peace in Zelizer, Craig. 2013. *Integrated Peacebuilding: Innovative Approaches to Transforming Conflict*. Boulder, CO: Westview Press.

51. Zelizer (2013), p. 110

In creating a World Beyond War, a gender-sensitive approach to our thinking and acting needs to be adopted. The following stages of engendering war prevention are required:[52]

- Making women visible as agents of change in preventing war and building peace
- Removing male bias in war prevention and peacebuilding data collection and research
- Rethinking drivers of war and peace to take gender into account
- Incorporating and mainstreaming gender into policy-making and practice

Photo: Inclusive Security / Young peacebuilders

Managing International and Civil Conflicts

The reactionary approaches and established institutions for managing international and civil conflicts have proven to be insufficient and often inadequate. We propose a series of improvements.

Shifting To A Pro-Active Posture

Dismantling the institutions of the War System and the beliefs and attitudes that underlie it will not be enough. An Alternative Global Security System needs to be constructed in its place. Much of this system is already in place, having evolved over the past hundred years, although either in embryonic form or in great need of strengthening. Some of it exists only in ideas that need to be institutionalized.

The existing parts of the system should not be seen as the static end-products of a peaceful world, but as elements of dynamic, imperfect processes of human evolution which leads to an increasingly nonviolent world with more equality for everyone. Only a pro-active posture will help strengthen the Alternative Global Security System.

Strengthening International Institutions and Regional Alliances

International institutions for managing conflict without violence have been evolving for a long time. A body of very functional international law has been developing for centuries and needs to be further developed to be an effective part of a peace system. In 1899 the International Court of Justice (ICJ; the "World Court") was set up to adjudicate disputes between nation states. The League of Nations followed in 1920. An association of 58 sovereign States, the League was based on the principle of collective security, that is, if a State committed aggression, the other states would either enact economic sanctions against that State or, as a last resort approach, provide military forces to defeat it. The League did settle some minor disputes and initiated global level peace building efforts. The problem was that the member states failed, in the main, to do what they said they would do, and so the aggressions of Japan, Italy, and Germany were not prevented, leading to World War II, the most destructive war in history. It is also noteworthy that the U.S. refused to join. After the Allied victory, the United

52. These points are modified from the four stages of engendering conflict resolution by Ramsbotham, Oliver, Hugh Miall, and Tom Woodhouse. 2016. *Contemporary Conflict Resolution: The Prevention, Management and Transformation of Deadly Conflicts*. 4th ed. Cambridge: Polity.)

Nations was set up as a new attempt at collective security. Also an association of sovereign states, the UN was supposed to resolve disputes and, where that was not feasible, the Security Council could decide to enact sanctions or provide a counter military force to deal with an aggressor state.

The UN also greatly expanded the peacebuilding initiatives begun by the League. However, the UN was hobbled by built-in structural constraints and the Cold War between the U.S. and the U.S.S.R. made meaningful cooperation difficult. The two superpowers also set up traditional military alliance systems aimed at one another, NATO and the Warsaw Pact.

Other regional alliance systems were also established. The European Union has kept a peaceful Europe despite differences, the African Union is keeping the peace between Egypt and Ethiopia, and the Association of South-East Asian Nations and the Union de Naciones Suramericanas are developing potential for its members and would-be members toward peace.

While international institutions for managing inter-state conflicts are a vital part of a peace system, the problems with both the League and the UN arose in part from a failure to dismantle the War System. They were set up within it and by themselves were unable to control war or arms races, etc. Some analysts believe that the problem is that they are associations of sovereign states which are committed, in the last resort (and sometimes earlier) to war as the arbiter of disputes. There are many ways that the UN as well as other international institutions can be constructively reformed to become more effective in keeping the peace including reforms of the Security Council, the General Assembly, peacekeeping forces and actions, funding, its relationship to non-government organizations and the addition of new functions.

Reforming the United Nations

The United Nations was created as a response to World War II to prevent war by negotiation, sanctions, and collective security. The Preamble to the Charter provides the overall mission:

> *To save succeeding generations from the scourge of war, which twice in our lifetime has brought untold sorrow to mankind, and to reaffirm faith in fundamental human rights, in the dignity and worth of the human person, in the equal rights of men and women and of nations large and small, and to establish conditions under which justice and respect for the obligations arising from treaties and other sources of international law can be maintained, and to promote social progress and better standards of life in larger freedom. . . .*

Reforming the United Nations can and needs to take place at different levels.

Reforming the Charter to More Effectively Deal with Aggression

The United Nations Charter does not outlaw war, it outlaws aggression. While the Charter does enable the Security Council to take action in the case of aggression, the doctrine of the so-called "responsibility to protect" is not found in it, and the selective justification of Western imperial adventures is a practice that must be ended. The UN Charter does not prohibit States from taking their own action in self-defense. Article 51 reads:

> *Nothing in the present Charter shall impair the inherent right of individual or collective self-defence if an armed attack occurs against a Member of the United Nations, until the Security Council has taken measures necessary to maintain international peace and security. Measures taken by Members in the exercise of this right of self-defence shall be immediately reported to the Security Council and shall not in any way affect the authority and responsibility of the Security Council under the present Charter to take at any time such action as it deems necessary in order to maintain or restore international peace and security.*

Further, nothing in the Charter requires the UN to take action and it does require the conflicting parties to first try to settle the dispute themselves by arbitration and next by action of any regional security system to which they belong. Only then is it up to the Security Council, which is often rendered impotent by the veto provision.

As desirable as it would be to outlaw forms of warfare including making war in self-defense, it is hard to see how that can be achieved until a fully developed peace system is in place. However, much progress can be made by changing the Charter to require the Security Council to take up any and all cases of violent conflict immediately upon their commencement and to immediately provide a course of action to halt hostilities by means of putting a ceasefire in place, to require mediation at the UN (with the aid of regional partners if desired), and if necessary to refer the dispute to the International Court of Justice. This will require several further reforms as listed below, including dealing with the veto, shifting to nonviolent methods as the primary tools by making use of nonviolent unarmed civilian peaceworkers, and providing an adequate (and adequately accountable) police power to enforce its decisions when needed.

It should be added that most wars in recent decades have been illegal under the UN Charter. However, there has been little awareness and no consequences for that fact.

Reforming the Security Council

Article 42 of the Charter gives the Security Council the responsibility for maintaining and restoring the peace. It is the only UN body with binding authority on member States. The Council does not have an armed force to carry out its decisions; rather, it has binding authority to call on the armed forces of member States. However the composition and methods of the Security Council are antiquated and only minimally effective in keeping or restoring the peace.

Composition

The Council is composed of 15 members, 5 of whom are permanent. These are the victorious powers in World War II (U.S., Russia, U.K., France, and China). They are also the members who have veto power. At the time of the writing in 1945, they demanded these conditions or would not have permitted the UN to come into being. These permanent five also claim and possess leading seats on the governing bodies of the major

committees of the UN, giving them a disproportionate and undemocratic amount of influence. They are also, along with Germany, as noted above, the major arms dealers to the world.

The world has changed dramatically in the intervening decades. The UN had gone from 50 members to 193, and population balances have changed dramatically as well. Further, the way in which Security Council seats are allotted by 4 regions is also unrepresentative with Europe and the UK having 4 seats while Latin America has only 1. Africa is also underrepresented. It is only rarely that a Muslim nation is represented on the Council. It is long past time to rectify this situation if the UN wants to command respect in these regions.

Also, the nature of the threats to peace and security has changed dramatically. At the time of the founding the current arrangement might have made sense given the need for great power agreement and that the main threat to peace and security was seen to be armed aggression. While armed aggression is still a threat – and permanent member the United States the worst recidivist – great military power is almost irrelevant to many of the new threats that exist today which include global warming, WMDs, mass movements of peoples, global disease threats, the arms trade and criminality.

One proposal is to increase the number of electoral regions to 9 in which each would have one permanent member and each region have 2 revolving members to add up to a Council of 27 seats, thus more perfectly reflecting national, cultural and population realities.

Revise or Eliminate the Veto

The veto is exercised over four types of decisions: the use of force to maintain or restore the peace, appointments to the Secretary-General's position, applications for membership, and amending the Charter and procedural matters which can prevent questions from even coming to the floor. Also, in the other bodies, the Permanent 5 tend to exercise a de facto veto. In Council, the veto has been used 265 times, primarily by the U.S. and the former Soviet Union, to block action, often rendering the UN impotent.

The veto hamstrings the Security Council. It is profoundly unfair in that it enables the holders to prevent any action against their own violations of the Charter's prohibition on aggression. It is also used as a favor in shielding their client states' misdeeds from Security Council actions. One proposal is to simply discard the veto. Another is to allow permanent members to cast a veto but to make three members casting it necessary to block passage of a substantive issue. Procedural issues should not be subject to the veto.

Other Necessary Reforms of the Security Council

Three procedures need to be added. Currently nothing requires the Security Council to act. At a minimum the Council should be required to take up all issues of threat to peace and security and decide whether to act on them or not ("The Duty to Decide"). Second is "The Requirement for Transparency." The Council should be required to disclose its reasons for deciding to or deciding not to take up the issue of a conflict. Further, the Council meets in secret about 98 percent of the time. At the least, its substantive deliberations need to be transparent. Third, the "Duty to Consult" would require the Council to take reasonable measures to consult with nations that would be impacted by its decisions.

Provide Adequate Funding

The UN's "Regular Budget" funds the General Assembly, Security Council, Economic and Social Council, the International Court of Justice, and special missions such as the UN Assistance Mission to Afghanistan. The Peacekeeping Budget is separate. Member states are assessed for both, rates depending on their GDP. The UN also receives voluntary donations which about equal the revenue from assessed funds.

Given its mission, the United Nations is grossly underfunded. The regular two-year budget for 2016 and 2017 is set at $5.4 billion and the Peacekeeping Budget for the fiscal year 2015-2016 is $8.27 billion, the total amounting to less than one half of one percent of global military expenditures (and about one percent of U.S. annual military related expenditures). Several proposals have been advanced to adequately fund the UN including a tax of a fraction of one percent on international financial transactions that could raise up to $300 billion to be applied primarily to UN development and environmental programs such as reducing child mortality, fighting epidemic diseases such as Ebola, countering the negative effects of climate change, etc.

Forecasting and Managing Conflicts Early On: A Conflict Management

Using the Blue Helmets, the UN is already stretched to fund 16 peacekeeping missions around the world, putting out or damping fires that could spread regionally or even globally.[53] While they are, at least in some cases, doing a good job under very difficult conditions, the UN needs to become far more proactive in foreseeing and preventing conflicts where possible, and quickly and nonviolently intervening in conflicts that have ignited in order to put out the fires quickly.

Forecasting

Maintain a permanent expert agency to monitor potential conflicts around the world and recommend immediate action to the Security Council or the Secretary General, beginning with:

Pro-active Mediation Teams

Maintain a permanent set of mediation experts qualified in language and cultural diversity and the latest techniques of non-adversarial mediation to be dispatched rapidly to states where either international aggression or civil war looks imminent. This has started with the so-called Standby Team of Mediation Experts who act as on-call advisers to peace envoys around the world on issues such as mediation strategy, power-sharing, constitution-making, human rights and natural resources.[54]

Align Early With Indigenous Nonviolent Movements

To date the UN has shown little understanding of the power that nonviolent movements within countries can exercise to prevent civil conflicts from becoming violent civil wars. At the least, the UN needs to be able to assist these movements by pressuring governments to avoid violent reprisals against them while bringing UN mediation teams to bear. The UN needs to engage with these movements. When this is deemed difficult due to concerns about infringing on national sovereignty, the UN can do the following.

---

53. See http://www.un.org/en/peacekeeping/operations/current.shtml for current peacekeeping missions

54. http://www.un.org/en/peacekeeping/operations/financing.shtml

Peacekeeping

The current UN Peacekeeping operations have major problems, including conflicting rules of engagement, lack of interaction with affected communities, lack of women, gender-based violence and failure to deal with the changing nature of warfare. A UN High-Level Independent Panel of Peace Operations, chaired by Nobel Peace Laureate Jose Ramos-Horta, recommended 4 essential shifts to UN peace operations: 1. Primacy of politics, that is political solutions must guide all UN peace operations. 2. Responsive operations, that is missions should be tailored to context and include the full spectrum of responses. 3. Stronger partnerships, that is developing resilient global and local peace and security architectures, 4. Field-focused and people-centered, that is a renewed resolve to serve and protect the people.[55]

According to Mel Duncan, co-founder of the Nonviolent Peaceforce, the panel also recognized that civilians can and do play an important role in the direct protection of civilians.

Improving and maintaining the current Blue Helmets peacekeeping operations and enhanced capability for long-term missions should be considered as the last resort approach and with increased accountability to a democratically reformed UN. To be clear, the operations of UN Peacekeeping or civilian protection operations are not what one would consider a military intervention for the sake of peace and security. The fundamental mission of international peacekeeping, policing or civilian protection authorized by the United Nations or another international body is different from military intervention. A military intervention is the introduction of outside military forces into an existing conflict through the introductions of arms, air strikes and combat troops to intervene in the conflict in order to influence a military outcome and defeat an enemy. It is the use of deadly force on a massive scale. UN Peacekeeping is guided by three basic principles: (1) consent of the parties; (2) impartiality; and (3) non-use of force except in self-defence and defence of the mandate. That is not to say, that civilian protection is being falsely used as a disguise for military interventions with less noble motives.

With that in mind, armed peacekeeping operations must be understood as a clear transitional step toward ultimately relying on more effective, viable nonviolent alternatives, in particular Unarmed Civilian Peacekeeping (UCP).

Rapid Reaction Force to Supplement the Blue Helmets

All peacekeeping missions must be approved by the Security Council. The UN's peacekeeping forces, the Blue Helmets, are recruited primarily from the developing nations. Several problems make them less effective than they could be. First, it takes several months to assemble a peacekeeping force, during which time the crisis can escalate dramatically. A standing, rapid reaction force which could intervene in a matter of days would solve this problem. Other problems with the Blue Helmets stem from using national forces and include: a disparity of participation, armaments, tactics, command and control, and rules of engagement.

Coordinate with Civilian-Based Nonviolent Intervention Agencies

Nonviolent, civilian-based peacekeeping teams have existed for over twenty years, including the largest, the Nonviolent Peaceforce (NP), headquartered in Brussels. The NP currently has observer status at the UN and participates in discussions of peacekeeping. These organizations, including not only NP but also Peace Brigades International, Christian Peacemaker Teams and others, can sometimes go where the UN cannot and thus can be effective in particular situations. The UN needs to

---

55. The Global Peace Operations Review is a web-portal providing analysis and data on peacekeeping operations and political missions. See the website at: http://peaceoperationsreview.org

encourage these activities and help fund them. The UN should cooperate with other INGOs such as International Alert, Search for Common Ground, the Muslim Voice for Peace, the Jewish Voice for Peace, the Fellowship of Reconciliation, and many others by enabling their efforts to intervene early on in conflict areas. In addition to funding those efforts through UNICEF or UNHCR, much more can be done in terms of including UCP in mandates and recognizing and promoting the methodologies.

Reform the General Assembly

The General Assembly (GA) is the most democratic of the UN bodies since it includes all the member States. It is concerned primarily with crucial peacebuilding programs. Then-Secretary General Kofi Annan suggested that the GA simplify its programs, abandon reliance on consensus since it results in watered-down resolutions, and adopt a supermajority for decision making. The GA needs to pay more attention to implementation and compliance with its decisions. It also needs a more efficient committee system and to involve civil society, that is NGOs, more directly in its work. Another problem with the GA is that it is composed of state members; thus a tiny state with 200,000 people has as much weight in voting as China or India.

A reform idea gaining popularity is to add to the GA a Parliamentary Assembly of members elected by the citizens of each country and in which the number of seats allocated to each country would more accurately reflect population and thus be more democratic. Then any decisions of the GA would have to pass both houses. Such "global MPs" would also be able to represent the common welfare of humanity in general rather than being required to follow the dictates of their governments back home as the current State ambassadors are.

Strengthen the International Court of Justice

The ICJ or "World Court" is the principal judicial body of the United Nations. It adjudicates cases submitted to it by the States and gives advisory opinions on legal matters referred to it by the UN and specialized agencies. Fifteen judges are elected for nine-year terms by the General Assembly and the Security Council. By signing the Charter, States undertake to abide by the decisions of the Court. Both State parties to a submission must agree in advance that the Court has jurisdiction if it is to accept their submission. Decisions are only binding if both parties agree in advance to abide by them. If, after this, in the rare event that a State party does not abide by the decision, the issue may be submitted to the Security Council for actions it deems are necessary to bring the State into compliance (potentially running into a Security Council veto).

The sources of the law on which the ICJ draws for its deliberations are treaties and conventions, judicial decisions, international custom, and the teachings of international law experts. The Court can only make determinations based on existing treaty or customary law since there is no body of legislative law (there being no world legislature). This makes for tortuous decisions. When the General Assembly asked for an advisory opinion on whether the threat or use of nuclear weapons is permitted under any circumstances in international law, the Court was unable to find any treaty law that permitted or forbade the threat or use. In the end, all it could do was suggest that customary law required States to continue to negotiate on a ban. Without a body of statutory law passed by a world legislative body, the Court is limited to existing treaties and customary law (which by definition is always behind the times) thus rendering it only mildly effective in some cases and all but useless in others.

Once again, the Security Council veto becomes a limit on the effectiveness of the Court. In the case of Nicaragua vs. The United States – the U.S. had mined Nicaragua's harbors in a clear act of war – the Court found against the U.S. whereupon the U.S. withdrew from compulsory jurisdiction (1986). When the matter was referred to the Security Council the U.S. exercised its veto to avoid penalty. In effect, the five permanent members can control the outcomes of the Court should it affect them or their allies. The Court needs to be independent of the Security Council veto. When a decision needs to be enforced by the Security Council against a member, that member must recuse itself according to the ancient principle of Roman Law: "No one shall be judge in his own case."

The Court has also been accused of bias, the judges voting not in the pure interests of justice but in the interests of the states that appointed them. While some of this is probably true, this criticism comes often from States that have lost their cases. Nevertheless, the more the Court follows rules of objectivity, the more weight its decisions will carry.

Cases involving aggression are usually brought not before the Court but before the Security Council, with all of its limitations. The Court needs the power to determine on its own if it has jurisdiction independent of the will of States and it then needs prosecutorial authority to bring States to the bar.

Strengthen the International Criminal Court

The International Criminal Court (ICC) is a permanent Court, created by a treaty, the "Rome Statute," which came into force on 1 July, 2002 after ratification by 60 nations. As of 2015 the treaty has been signed by 122 nations (the "States Parties"), although not by India and China. Three States have declared they do not intend to become a part of the Treaty—Israel, the Republic of Sudan, and the United States. The Court is free standing and is not a part of the UN System although it operates in partnership with it. The Security Council may refer cases to the Court, although the Court is under no obligation to investigate them. Its jurisdiction is strictly limited to crimes against humanity, war crimes, genocide, and crimes of aggression as these have been strictly defined within the tradition of international law and as they are explicitly set out in the Statute. It is a Court of the last resort. As a general principle, the ICC may not exercise jurisdiction before a State Party has had an opportunity to try the alleged crimes itself and demonstrate capability and genuine willingness to do so, that is, the courts of the States Parties must be functional. The court is "complementary to national criminal jurisdiction" (Rome Statute, Preamble). If the Court determines that it has jurisdiction, that determination may be challenged and any investigation suspended until the challenge is heard and a determination is made. The Court may not exercise jurisdiction on the territory of any State not signatory to the Rome Statute.

The ICC is composed of four organs: the Presidency, the Office of the Prosecutor, the Registry and the Judiciary which is made up of eighteen judges in three Divisions: Pre-trial, Trial, and Appeals.

The Court has come under several different criticisms. First, it has been accused of unfairly singling out atrocities in Africa while those elsewhere have been ignored. As of 2012, all seven open cases focused on African leaders. The Permanent Five of the Security Council appear to lean in the direction of this bias. As a principle, the Court must be able to demonstrate impartiality. However, two factors mitigate this criticism: 1) more African nations are party to the treaty than other nations; and 2) the Court has in fact pursued criminal allegations in Iraq and Venezuela (which did not lead to prosecutions).

A second and related criticism is that the Court appears to some to be a function of neo-colonialism as the funding and staffing are imbalanced toward the European Union and Western States. This can be addressed by spreading out the funding and the recruitment of expert staff from other nations.

Third, it has been argued that the bar for qualification of judges needs to be higher, requiring expertise in international law and prior trial experience. It is unquestionably desirable that the judges be of the highest caliber possible and have such experience. Whatever obstacles stand in the way of meeting this high standard need to be addressed.

Fourth, some argue that the powers of the Prosecutor are too broad. It should be pointed out that these were established by the Statute and would require amending to be changed. In particular, some have argued that the Prosecutor should not have a right to indict persons whose nations are not signatory; however, this appears to be a misunderstanding as the Statute limits indictment to signatories or other nations which have agreed to an indictment even if they are not signatory.

Fifth, there is no appeal to a higher court. Note that the Pre-trial chamber of the Court must agree, based on evidence, that an indictment can be made, and a defendant can appeal its findings to the Appeals Chamber. Such a case was successfully maintained by an accused in 2014 and the case dropped. However, it might be worth considering the creation of an appeals court outside of the ICC.

Sixth, there are legitimate complaints about lack of transparency. Many of the Courts sessions and proceedings are held in secret. While there may be legitimate reasons for some of this (protection of witnesses, inter alia), the highest degree of transparency possible is required and the Court needs to review its procedures in this regard.

Seventh, some critics have argued that the standards of due process are not up to the highest standards of practice. If this is the case, it must be corrected.

Eighth, others have argued that the Court has achieved too little for the amount of money it has spent, having obtained only one conviction to date. This, however is an argument for the Court's respect for process and its inherently conservative nature. It has clearly not gone on witch hunts for every nasty person in the world but has shown admirable restraint. It is also a testimony to the difficulty of bringing these prosecutions, assembling evidence sometimes years after the fact of massacres and other atrocities, especially in a multicultural setting.

Finally, the heaviest criticism laid against the Court is its very existence as a transnational institution. Some don't like or want it for what it is, an implied limitation on unconfined State sovereignty. But so, too, is every treaty, and they are all, including the Rome Statute, entered into voluntarily and for the common good. Ending war cannot be achieved by sovereign states alone. The record of millennia shows nothing but failure in that regard. Transnational judicial institutions are a necessary part of an Alternative Global Security System. Of course the Court must be subject to the same norms which they would advocate for the rest of the global community, that is, transparency, accountability, speedy and due process, and highly qualified personnel. The establishment of the International Criminal Court was a major step forward in the construction of a functioning peace system.

It needs to be emphasized that the ICC is a brand-new institution, the first iteration of an international community's efforts to assure that the world's most egregious criminals do not get away with their mass crimes. Even the United Nations, which is the second iteration of collective security, is still evolving and still in need of serious reform.

Photo: Trained nonviolent civilian peacekeepers from the Nonviolent Peaceforce and Peace Brigades International

Civil society organizations are at the forefront of reform efforts. The Coalition for the International Criminal Court consists of 2,500 civil society organizations in 150 countries advocating for a fair, effective, and independent ICC and improved access to justice for victims of genocide, war crimes and crimes against humanity. The American Non-Governmental Organizations Coalition for the International Criminal Court is a coalition of non-governmental organizations committed to achieving through education, information, promotion and an aroused public opinion full United States support for the International Criminal Court and the earliest possible U.S. ratification of the Court's Rome Statute.[56]

Nonviolent Intervention: Civilian Peacekeeping Forces

Trained, nonviolent and unarmed civilian forces have for over twenty years been invited to intervene in conflicts around the world to provide protection for human rights defenders and peace workers by maintaining a high profile physical presence accompanying threatened individuals and organizations. Since these organizations are not associated with any government, and since their personnel are drawn from many countries and have no agenda other than creating a safe space where dialogue can occur between conflicting parties, they have a credibility that national governments lack.

By being nonviolent and unarmed they present no physical threat to others and can go where armed peacekeepers might provoke a violent clash. They provide an open space, dialogue with government authorities and armed forces, and create a link between local peace workers and the international community. Initiated by Peace Brigades International in 1981, PBI has current projects in Guatemala, Honduras, New Mexico, Nepal and Kenya. The Nonviolent Peaceforce was founded in 2000 and is headquartered in Brussels. NP has four goals for its work: to create a space for lasting peace, to protect civilians, to develop and promote the theory and practice of unarmed civilian peacekeeping so that it may be adopted as a policy option by decision makers and public institutions, and to build the pool of professionals able to join peace teams through regional activities, training, and maintaining a roster of trained, available people. NP currently has teams in the Philippines, Myanmar, South Sudan, and Syria.

For example, the Nonviolent Peaceforce currently operates its largest project in civil-war South Sudan. Unarmed civilian protectors successfully accompany women collecting firewood in conflict zones, where fighting parties use rape as a weapon of war. Three or four unarmed civilian protectors have proven to be 100% successful in preventing those forms of wartime rape. Mel Duncan, co-founder of the Nonviolent Peaceforce recounts another example of South Sudan:

> [Derek and Andreas] were with 14 women and children, when the area where they were with these people was attacked by a militia. They took the 14 women and children in a tent, while people outside were shot point blank. On three occasions, rebel militia came to Andreas and Derek and pointed AK47s at their heads and said 'you have to go, we want those people'. And on all three occasions, very calmly, Andreas and Derek held up their Nonviolent Peaceforce identity badges and said: "we are unarmed, we are here to protect civilians, and we will not leave'. After the third time the militia left, and the people were spared. (Mel Duncan)

---

56. http://www.iccnow.org/; http://www.amicc.org/

Such stories bring up the question of risk to unarmed civilian peacekeepers. One certainly cannot create a more threatening scenario than the previous one. Yet Nonviolent Peaceforce has had five conflict related injuries - three of which were accidental - in thirteen years of operating. Moreover, it is safe to assume that an armed protection in the example described would have resulted in the deaths of Derek and Andreas as well as those they sought to protect.

These and other organizations such as Christian Peacemaker Teams provide a model that can be scaled up to take the place of armed peacekeepers and other forms of violent intervention. They are a perfect example of the role civil society is already playing in keeping the peace. Their intervention goes beyond intervention through presence and dialog processes to working on the reconstruction of the social fabric in conflict zones.

To date, these crucial efforts are under recognized and underfunded. They need to be fully sanctioned by the UN and other institutions and by international law. These are among the most promising efforts to protect civilians and create space for civil society and contribute to lasting peace.

International Law

International Law has no defined area or governing body. It is composed of many laws, rules, and customs governing the relations between different nations, their governments, businesses, and organizations.

It includes a piecemeal collection of customs; agreements; treaties; accords, charters such as the United Nations Charter; protocols; tribunals; memorandums; legal precedents of the International Court of Justice and more. Since there is no governing, enforcing entity, it is a largely voluntary endeavor. It includes both common law and case law. Three main principles govern international law. They are Comity (where two nations share common policy ideas, one will submit to the judicial decisions of the other); Act of State Doctrine (based on sovereignty—one State's judicial bodies will not question the policies of another State or interfere with its foreign policy); and the Doctrine of Sovereign Immunity (preventing a State's nationals from being tried in the courts of another State).

The chief problem of international law is that, being based on the anarchic principle of national sovereignty, it cannot deal very effectively with the global commons, as the failure to bring concerted action to bear on climate shift demonstrates. While it has become obvious in terms of peace and environmental dangers that we are one people forced to live together on a small, fragile planet, there is no legal entity capable of enacting statutory law, and so we must rely on negotiating ad hoc treaties to deal with problems that are systematic. Given that it is unlikely such an entity will develop in the near future, we need to strengthen the treaty regime.

Encourage Compliance With Existing Treaties

Crucial treaties for controlling war that are now in force are not recognized by a few critical nations. In particular, the Convention on the Prohibition of the Use, Stockpiling, Production and Transfer of Anti-Personnel Mines and on their Destruction is not recognized by the United States, Russia and China. The Rome Statute of the International Criminal Court is not recognized by the United States, Sudan, and Israel. Russia has not ratified it. India and China are holdouts, as are a number of other members of the UN. While hold out States argue that the court might be biased against them, the only plausible reason for a nation not becoming a party to the Statute is that it reserves the right

to commit war crimes, genocide, crimes against humanity or aggression, or to define such acts as not coming under the common definitions of such acts. These States must be pressured by global citizens to come to the table and play by the same rules as the rest of humanity. States must also be pressured to comply with human rights law and with the various Geneva Conventions. The non-complying states, including the U.S., need to ratify the Comprehensive Test Ban Treaty and reassert the validity of the still-in force Kellogg-Briand Pact which outlaws war.

Create New Treaties

The evolving situation will always require the consideration of new treaties, the legal relations between the different parties. Three that should be taken up immediately are:

Control Greenhouse Gases

New treaties are necessary to deal with global climate shift and its consequences, in particular a treaty governing the emission of all greenhouse gases that includes assistance for the developing nations.

Pave the Way for Climate Refugees

A related but separate treaty will need to deal with the rights of climate refugees to migrate both internally and internationally. This applies to the urgency of the already ongoing effects of climate change, but also the the current refugees crisis emerging from the Middle East and North Africa, where historical and current Western policies contributed immensely to war and violence. As long as war exists, there will be refugees. The United Nations Convention on Refugees legally obligates signatories to take in refugees. This provision requires compliance but given the overwhelming numbers that will be involved, it needs to include provisions for assistance if major conflicts are to be avoided. This assistance could be part of a Global Development Plan as described below.

Establish Truth and Reconciliation Commissions

When interstate or civil war occurs in spite of the many barriers the Alternative Global Security System throws up, the various mechanisms outlined above will work quickly to bring an end to overt hostilities, restoring order. Following that, paths to reconciliation are necessary to ensure that there is no relapse into direct and indirect violence. The following processes are considered necessary for reconciliation:

- Uncovering the truth of what happened
- Acknowledgement by the offender(s) of harm done
- Remorse expressed in apology for victim(s)
- Forgiveness
- Justice in some form
- Planning to prevent recurrence
- Resuming constructive aspects of the relationship
- Rebuilding trust over time[57]

57. Santa-Barbara, Joanna. 2007. "Reconciliation." In *Handbook of Peace and Conflict Studies*, edited by Charles Webel and Johan Galtung, 173–86. New York: Routledge.

Truth and Reconciliation Commissions are a form of transitional justice and offer a path alternative to prosecutions and counteract cultures of denial.[58] They have been set up in more than 20 countries. Such commissions have already worked in many situations in Ecuador, Canada, the Czech Republic, etc., and most notably in South Africa at the end of the Apartheid regime.[59] Such commissions take the place of criminal proceedings and act to begin to restore trust so that genuine peace, rather than a simple cessation of hostilities, can actually commence. Their function is to establish the facts of past wrongdoing by all actors, both the injured and the perpetrators (who may confess in return for clemency) in order to prevent any historical revisionism and to remove any causes for a new outbreak of violence motivated by revenge. Other potential benefits are: public and official exposure of truth contributes to social and personal healing; engage all of society in national dialog; look at ills of society that made abuses possible; and sense of public ownership in the process.[60]

Create a Stable, Fair and Sustainable Global Economy as a Foundation for Peace

War, economic injustice and failure of sustainability are tied together in many ways, not the least of which is high youth unemployment in volatile regions such as the Middle East, where it creates a seed bed for growing extremists. And the global, oil-based economy is an obvious cause of militarized conflict and imperial ambitions to project power and protect U.S. access to foreign resources. The imbalance between the affluent northern economies and the poverty of the global south can be righted by a Global Aid Plan that takes into account the need to conserve ecosystems upon which economies rest and by democratizing the international economic institutions including the World Trade Organization, the International Monetary Fund and the International Bank for Reconstruction and Development.

There is no polite way to say that business is destroying the world.

Paul Hawken (Environmentalist, Author)

Political economist Lloyd Dumas states, "a militarized economy distorts and ultimately weakens society". He outlines the basic principles of a peacekeeping economy.[61] These are:

Establish balanced relationships – everyone gains benefit at least equal to their contribution and there is little incentive to disrupt the relationship. Example: The European Union – they debate, there are conflicts, but there are no threats of war within the EU.

Emphasize development – Most of the wars since WWII have been fought in developing countries. Poverty and missing opportunities are breeding grounds for violence. Development is an effective counter-terrorism strategy, as it weakens the support network for terrorist groups. Example: Recruitment of young, uneducated males in urban areas into terror organizations.[62]

58. Fischer, Martina. 2015. "Transitional Justice and Reconciliation: Theory and Practice." In *The Contemporary Conflict Resolution Reader*, edited by Hugh Miall, Tom Woodhouse, Oliver Ramsbotham, and Christopher Mitchell, 325–33. Cambridge: Polity.

59. Reconciliation through Restorative Justice: Analyzing South Africa's Truth and Reconciliation Process - http://www.beyondintractability.org/library/reconciliation-through-restorative-justice-analyzing-south-africas-truth-and-reconciliation

60. Fischer, Martina. 2015. "Transitional Justice and Reconciliation: Theory and Practice." In *The Contemporary Conflict Resolution Reader*, edited by Hugh Miall, Tom Woodhouse, Oliver Ramsbotham, and Christopher Mitchell, 325–33. Cambridge: Polity.

61. Dumas, Lloyd J. 2011. *The Peacekeeping Economy: Using Economic Relationships to Build a More Peaceful, Prosperous, and Secure World.*

62. Supported by the following study: Mousseau, Michael. "Urban Poverty and Support for Islamist Terror Survey

Minimize ecological stress – The competition for depletable resources ("stress-generating resources") – most notably oil and water – generates dangerous conflicts between nations and groups within nations.

It is proven that war is more likely to happen where there is oil.[63] Using natural resources more efficiently, developing and using non-polluting technologies and procedures and a large shift toward qualitative rather than quantitative economic growth can reduce ecological stress.

Democratize International Economic Institutions (WTO, IMF, IBRD)

The global economy is administered, financed and regulated by three institutions – The World Trade Organization (WTO), The International Monetary Fund (IMF), and the International Bank for Reconstruction and Development (IBRD; "World Bank"). The problem with these bodies is that they are undemocratic and favor the rich nations against the poorer nations, unduly restrict environmental and labor protections, and lack transparency, discourage sustainability, and encourage resource extraction and dependence.[64] The unelected and unaccountable governing board of the WTO can override the labor and environmental laws of nations, rendering the populace vulnerable to exploitation and environmental degradation with its various health implications.

> *The current form of corporate-dominated globalization is escalating the plunder of the earth's riches, increasing the exploitation of workers, expanding police and military repression and leaving poverty in its wake.*

Sharon Delgado (Author, Director Earth Justice Ministries)

Globalization itself is not the issue—it's free trade. The complex of government elites and transnational corporations that control these institutions are driven by an ideology of Market Fundamentalism or "Free Trade," a euphemism for one-sided trade in which wealth flows from the poor to the rich. The legal and financial systems these institutions set up and enforce allow for the export of industry to havens of pollution in countries that oppress workers who attempt to organize for decent wages, health, safety and environmental protections. The manufactured goods are exported back to the developed countries as consumer goods. The costs are externalized to the poor and the global environment. As the less developed nations have gone deeply into debt under this regime, they are required to accept IMF "austerity plans," that destroy their social safety nets creating a class of powerless, impoverished workers for the northern-owned factories. The regime also impacts agriculture. Fields that ought to be growing food for people are instead growing flowers for the cut-flower trade in Europe and the U.S. Or they have been taken over by elites, the subsistence farmers shoved out, and they grow corn or raise cattle for export to the global north. The poor

Results of Muslims in Fourteen Countries." *Journal of Peace Research* 48, no. 1 (January 1, 2011): 35–47. This assertion should not be confused with an overly simplistic interpretation of the multiple root causes of terrorism

63. Supported by the following study: Bove, V., Gleditsch, K. S., & Sekeris, P. G. (2015). "Oil above Water" Economic Interdependence and Third-party Intervention. *Journal of Conflict Resolution.* Key findings are: Foreign governments are 100 times more likely to intervene in civil wars when the country at war has large oil reserves. Oil dependent economies have favored stability and support dictators rather than emphasizing democracy. http://communication.warpreventioninitiative.org/?p=240

64. For some, the underlying assumptions of the economic theory need to be questioned. For example, the organization Positive Money (http://positivemoney.org/) aims to build a movement for a fair, democratic and sustainable money system by taking the power to create money away from the banks and return it to a democratic and accountable process, by creating money free od debt, and by putting new money into the real economy rather than financial markets and property bubbles.

drift into the mega-cities where, if lucky, they find work in the oppressive factories creating export goods. The injustice of this regime creates resentment and calls for revolutionary violence which then calls out police and military repression. The police and military are often trained in crowd suppression by the United States military at the "Western Hemisphere Institute for Security Cooperation" (formerly "School of the Americas"). At this institution training includes advanced combat arms, psychological operations, military intelligence and commando tactics.[65] All of this is destabilizing and creates more insecurity in the world.

The solution requires policy changes and a moral awakening in the north. The obvious first move is to cease training police and military for dictatorial regimes. Second, the governing boards of these international financial institutions need to be democratized. They are now dominated by the Industrial North nations. Third, so-called "free trade" policies need to be replaced with fair trade policies. All of this requires a moral shift, from selfishness on the part of Northern consumers who often purchase only the cheapest possible goods regardless of who suffers, to a sense of global solidarity and a realization that damage to ecosystems anywhere has global implications, and has blow-back for the north, most obviously in terms of climate deterioration and immigration problems that lead to militarizing borders. If people can be assured of a decent life in their own countries, they will not be likely to try to immigrate illegally.

Create an Environmentally Sustainable Global Aid Plan

Development reinforces diplomacy and defense, reducing long-term threats to our national security by helping build stable, prosperous and peaceful societies.

2006 United States National Security Strategy Plan.

A related solution to democratizing the international economic institutions is to institute a Global Aid Plan to achieve stabilizing economic and environmental justice worldwide.[66] The goals would be similar to the UN Millennium Development Goals to end poverty and hunger, develop local food security, provide education and health care, and to achieve these goals by creating stable, efficient, sustainable economic development that does not exacerbate climate shift. It will also need to provide funds to assist with the resettlement of climate refugees. The Plan would be administered by a new, international non-governmental organization to prevent it from becoming a foreign policy tool of rich nations. It would be funded by a dedication of 2-5 percent of GDP from the advanced industrial nations for twenty years. For the U.S. this amount would be approximately a few hundred billion dollars, far less than is the $1.3 trillion currently spent on the failed national security system. The plan would be administered at ground level by an International Peace and Justice Corps made up of volunteers. It would require strict accounting and transparency from the recipient governments to ensure that the aid actually got to the people.

A Proposal For Starting Over: A Democratic, Citizens Global Parliament

The United Nations ultimately needs such serious reforms that it can be useful to think of them in terms of replacing the United Nations with a more effective body, one that can actually keep (or help to create) the peace. This understanding is rooted in the

---

65. For more information see School of the Americas Watch at www.soaw.org

66. Somewhat similar, the so-called Marshall Plan was a post World War II American economic initiative to help rebuild European economies. See more at: https://en.wikipedia.org/wiki/Marshall_Plan

failures of the UN which may stem from inherent problems with collective security as a model for keeping or restoring the peace.

Inherent Problems With Collective Security

The United Nations is based on the principle of collective security, that is, when a nation threatens or initiates aggression, the other nations will bring to bear preponderant force acting as a deterrent, or as a very early remedy for an invasion by defeating the aggressor on the battlefield. This is, of course, a militarized solution, threatening or carrying out a larger war to deter or prevent a smaller war. The one principal example – the Korean War – was a failure. The war dragged on for years and the border remains heavily militarized. In fact, the war has never been formally terminated. Collective security is simply a tweaking of the existing system of using violence to attempt to counter violence. It actually requires a militarized world so that the world body has armies it can call on. Moreover, while the UN is theoretically based on this system, it is not designed to execute it, since it has no duty to do so in the event of conflicts. It has only an opportunity to act and that is severely enervated by the Security Council veto. Five privileged member states can, and very often have, exercised their own national aims rather than agreed to cooperate for the common good. This partially explains why the UN has failed to stop so many wars since its founding. This, along with its other weaknesses, explains why some people think humanity needs to start over with a far more democratic institution that has the power to enact and enforce statutory law and bring about peaceful resolution of conflicts.

The Earth Federation

The following is based on the argument that reforms to existing international institutions are important, but not necessarily enough. It is an argument that the existing institutions for dealing with international conflict and the larger problems of humankind are wholly inadequate and that world needs to start over with a new global organization: the "Earth Federation," governed by a democratically elected World Parliament and with a World Bill of Rights. The United Nations' failures are due to its very nature as a body of sovereign states; it is unable to solve the several problems and planetary crises which humankind is now facing. Instead of requiring disarmament, the UN requires the nation states to maintain military force that they can loan to the UN on demand. The UN's last resort is to use war to stop war, an oxymoronic idea. Furthermore, the UN has no legislative powers—it cannot enact binding laws. It can only bind nations to go to war to stop a war. It is totally unequipped to solve global environmental problems (the United Nations Environment Programme has not stopped deforestation, toxification, climate change, fossil fuel use, global soil erosion, pollution of the oceans, etc.). The UN has failed to solve the problem of development; global poverty remains acute. Existing development organizations, especially the International Monetary Fund and the International Bank for Reconstruction and Development (the "World Bank") and the various international "free" trade agreements, have simply allowed the rich to fleece the poor. The World Court is impotent, it has no power to bring disputes before it; they can only be brought voluntarily by the parties themselves, and there is no way to enforce its decisions. The General Assembly is impotent; it can only study and recommend. It has no power to change anything. Adding a parliamentary body to it would just be creating a body which would recommend to the recommending body. The world's problems are now at a crisis and are not amenable to being solved by an anarchy of competitive, armed sovereign nation states each interested only in pursuing its national interest and unable to act for the common good.

Therefore, reforms of the United Nations must move toward or be followed by the creation of an unarmed, non-military Earth Federation, made up of a democratically

elected World Parliament with power to pass binding legislation, a World Judiciary, and a World Executive as the administrative body. A large movement of citizens has met several times as the Provisional World Parliament and they have drafted a draft World Constitution designed to protect liberty, human rights, and the global environment, and to provide for prosperity for all.

The Role of Global Civil Society and International Non-government Organizations

Civil society usually encompasses actors in professional associations, clubs, unions, faith-based organizations, nongovernmental organizations, clans, and other community groups.[67] Those are mostly found on a local/national level and together with global civil society networks and campaigns, they form an unprecedented infrastructure to challenge war and militarism.

In 1900 there were a handful of global civil institutions such as the International Postal Union and the Red Cross. In the century and some since, there has been an astonishing rise of international non-governmental organizations devoted to peace-building and peacekeeping. There are now thousands of these INGOs including such organizations as: the Nonviolent Peaceforce, Greenpeace, Servicio Paz y Justicia, Peace Brigades International, the Women's International League for Peace and Freedom, Veterans for Peace, the Fellowship of Reconciliation, the Hague Appeal for Peace, the International Peace Bureau, Muslim Peacemaker Teams, Jewish Voice for Peace, Oxfam International, Doctors Without Borders, Pace e Bene, Ploughshares Fund, Apopo, Citizens for Global Solutions, Nukewatch, the Carter Center, the Conflict Resolution Center International, the Natural Step, Transition Towns, United Nations Association, Rotary International, Women's Action for New Directions, Peace Direct, the American Friends Service Committee, and countless other smaller and less well known ones such as the Blue Mountain Project or the War Prevention Initiative. The Nobel Peace Committee recognized the importance of global civil society organizations, awarding several of them with the Nobel Peace Prize.

A heartening example is the founding of Combatants for Peace:

> *The "Combatants for Peace" movement was started jointly by Palestinians and Israelis, who have taken an active part in the cycle of violence; Israelis as soldiers in the Israeli army (IDF) and Palestinians as part of the violent struggle for Palestinian freedom. After brandishing weapons for so many years, and having seen one another only through weapon sights, we have decided to put down our guns, and to fight for peace.*

We can also look at how individuals like Jody Williams harnessed the power of global citizen-diplomacy to help the international community agree on the global ban on land-mines or how a delegation of citizen-diplomats are building people-to-people bridges between Russians and Americans amidst heightened international tensions in 2016.[68]

These individuals and organizations knit the world together into a pattern of care and concern, opposing war and injustice, working for peace and justice and a sustainable economy.[69] These organizations are not only advocates for peace, they work on the ground to successfully mediate, resolve, or transform conflicts and build peace. They are recognized as a global force for good. Many are accredited to the United Nations. Aided by the World Wide Web, they are the proof of an emerging consciousness of planetary citizenship.

---

67. See Paffenholz, T. (2010). *Civil society & peacebuilding: a critical assessment.* The case studies in this book examines the role of civil society peacebuilding efforts in conflict zones such as Northern Ireland, Cyprus, Israel and Palestine, Afghanistan, Sri Lanka, and Somalia.

68. The Center for Citizen Initiatives (http://ccisf.org/) began a series citizen-to-citizen initiatives and exchanges, buttressed by official media PR and social media networks across the United States and Russia. See also the book: *The Power of Impossible Ideas: Ordinary Citizens' Extraordinary Efforts to Avert International Crisis.* 2012. Odenwald Press.

69. For more, see the book on the development of the huge, unnamed movement *Blessed Unrest* (2007) by Paul Hawken.

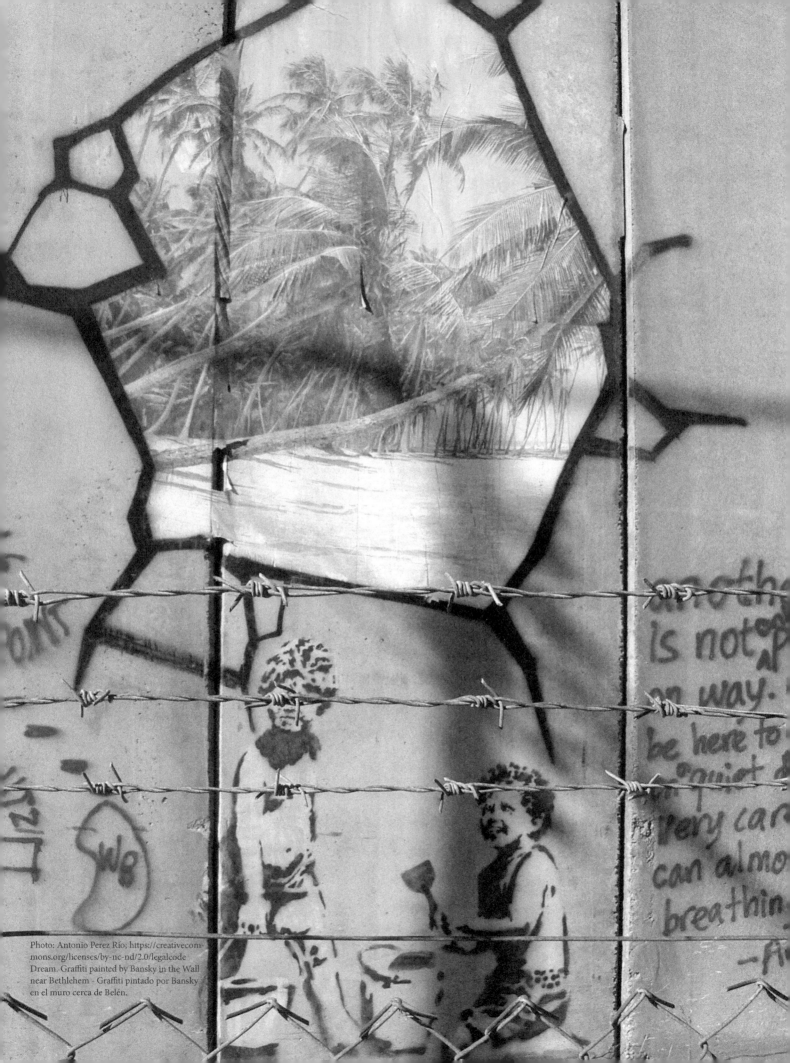

CREATING A CULTURE OF PEACE

The foregoing material might be likened to the hardware of an Alternative Global Security System. It dealt with the actual hardware of war and the institutions that support it and institutional reforms necessary to manage conflict without large-scale interstate or civil violence. The following material is the necessary software to run it. It addresses what Thomas Merton called the "climate of thought" that allows politicians and everyone else to prepare for and carry out massive violence.

> *Put in the simplest possible terms, a peace culture is a culture that promotes peaceable diversity. Such a culture includes lifeways, patterns of belief, values, behavior, and accompanying institutional arrangements that promote mutual caring and well-being as well as an equality that includes appreciation of difference, stewardship, and equitable sharing of the resources. . . . It offers mutual security for humankind in all its diversity through a profound sense of species identity as well as kinship with the living earth. There is no need for violence.*

Elise Boulding (Founding figure of Peace and Conflict Studies)

A culture of peace is contrasted with a warrior culture, also known as a dominator society, where warrior gods instruct the people to create hierarchies of rank so that men dominate other men, men dominate women, there is constant competition and frequent physical violence and nature is seen as something to be conquered. In a warrior culture, safety is only for those individuals or nations that are at the top, if they can stay there. No society is completely one or the other, but in today's world the tilt is toward the warrior societies, making necessary the growth of a culture of peace if humanity is to survive. Societies that socialize their children for aggressive behavior make wars more likely, and in a vicious circle, wars socialize people for aggression.

> *Every relationship of domination, of exploitation, of oppression is by definition violent, whether or not the violence is expressed by drastic means. In such a relationship, dominator and dominated alike are reduced to things – the former dehumanized by an excess of power, the latter by a lack of it. And things cannot love.*

Paulo Freire (Educator)

In 1999 the United Nations General Assembly approved a Programme of Action on a Culture of Peace.[1] Article I further defines it:

A culture of peace is a set of values, attitudes, traditions and modes of behaviour and ways of life based on:

1. *Respect for life, ending of violence and promotion and practice of nonviolence through education, dialogue and cooperation;*
2. *Full respect for the principles of sovereignty, territorial integrity and political independence of States and non-intervention in matters which are essentially within the domestic jurisdiction of any State, in accordance with the Charter of the United Nations and international law;*
3. *Full respect for and promotion of all human rights and fundamental freedoms;*
4. *Commitment to peaceful settlement of conflicts;*
5. *Efforts to meet the developmental and environmental needs of present and future generations;*
6. *Respect for and promotion of the right to development;*
7. *Respect for and promotion of equal rights and opportunities for women and men;*
8. *Respect for and promotion of the right of everyone to freedom of expression, opinion and information;*
9. *Adherence to the principles of freedom, justice, democracy, tolerance, solidarity, cooperation, pluralism, cultural diversity, dialogue and understanding at all levels of society and among nations; fostered by an enabling*

The General Assembly identified eight action areas:

1. *Fostering a culture of peace through education*
2. *Promoting sustainable economic and social development.*
3. *Promoting respect for all human rights.*
4. *Ensuring equality between women and men.*
5. *Fostering democratic participation.*
6. *Advancing understanding, tolerance and solidarity.*
7. *Supporting participatory communication and the free flow of information and knowledge.*
8. *Promoting international peace and security.*

The Global Movement for the Culture of Peace is a partnership of groups from civil society that have banded together to promote a culture of peace. Part of the work is to tell a new story.

Telling a New Story

The deepest crises experienced by any society are those moments of change when the story becomes inadequate for meeting the survival demands of a present situation.

Thomas Berry ("Earth Scholar")

Crucial to further developing a culture of peace is the telling of a new story about humanity and the earth. The old story, beloved by governments and too many journalists **63**

---

1. The valuable ideals of the United Nations and its Culture of Peace initiative need to be acknowledged despite the UN's organizational imperfection outlined earlier.

and teachers, is that the world is a dangerous place, that war has always been with us, is inevitable, in our genes, and good for the economy, that preparing for war ensures peace, that it's impossible to end war, that the global economy is a dog-eat-dog competition and if you don't win you lose, that resources are scarce and if you want to live well you must grab them, often by force, and that nature is simply a mine of raw materials. This story is a fatalistic self-fulfilling deterministic outlook that claims to be realism but is in fact defeatist pessimism.

In the old story, history is presented as little more than a succession of wars. As peace educator Darren Reiley puts it:

> *The assumption that war is a natural and necessary force of human progress is deeply ingrained and continues to be reinforced by the way we teach history. In the U.S., the content standards for teaching American History go like this: "Cause and consequences of the American Revolutionary War, the War of 1812, the Civil War, World War I, the Great Depression (and how World War II ended it), Civil Rights, war, war, war." Taught this way, war becomes the unquestioned driver of social change, but it is an assumption that needs to be challenged, or students will take it for the truth.*

All the cooperative endeavors of humanity, the long periods of peace, the existence of peaceful societies, the development of conflict resolution skills, the remarkable stories of successful nonviolence, are all ignored in the traditional recounting of the past that can only be described as "warist." Fortunately, historians from the Council on Peace Research in History and others have begun revising this view, bringing to light the reality of peace in our history.

There is a new story, backed up by science and experience. In fact, war is a relatively recent social invention. We humans have been around for over 100,000 years but there is little evidence for warfare, and certainly interstate warfare, going back much more than 6,000 years, very few known earlier instances of war back 12,000 years, and none earlier.[2] For 95 percent of our history we were without war, indicating that war is not genetic, but cultural. Even during the worst period of wars we have seen, the 20th century, there was far more interstate peace in the human community than war. For example, the U.S. fought Germany for six years but was at peace with her for ninety-four, with Australia for over a hundred years, with Canada for well over that, and never at war with Brazil, Norway, France, Poland, Burma, etc. Most people live at peace most of the time. In fact, we are living in the midst of a developing global peace system.

The old story defined the human experience in terms of materialism, greed, and violence in a world where individuals and groups are alienated from one another and from nature. The new story is a story of belonging, of cooperative relationships. Some have called it the story of a developing "partnership society." It is the story of an emerging realization that we are a single species –humanity — living in a generous web of life that provides all we need for life. We are partnered with one another and with the earth for life. What enriches life is not mere material goods, although a minimum is surely necessary—but rather meaningful work and relationships based on trust and mutual service. Acting together we have the power to create our own destiny. We are not doomed to failure.

---

2. There is not one single authoritative source providing evidence for the birth of warfare. Numerous archeological and anthropological studies provide ranges from 12,000 to 6,000 year or less. It would go beyond the scope of this report to enter the debate. A good overview of selected sources is provided by John Horgan in *The End of War* (2012)

The Metta Center on Nonviolence holds four propositions that help define the new story.

- Life is an interconnected whole of inestimable worth.
- We cannot be fulfilled by an indefinite consumption of things, but by a potentially infinite expansion of our relationships.
- We can never injure others without injuring ourselves . . .
- Security does not come from . . . defeating "enemies"; it can only come from . . . turning enemies into friends.[3]

The Unprecedented Peace Revolution of Modern Times

Surprisingly, if one looks at the last 200 years of history, one sees not only the industrialization of warfare, but also a powerful trend toward a peace system and the development of a culture of peace, a veritable revolution. Beginning with the emergence for the first time in history of citizen based organizations dedicated to getting rid of war in the early 19th century, some 28 trends are clearly visible leading toward a developing global peace system. These include: the emergence for the first time of international courts (starting with the International Court of Justice in 1899); of international parliamentary institutions to control war (the League in 1919 and the UN in 1946); the invention of international peacekeeping forces under the auspices of the UN (Blue Helmets) and other international organizations such as the African Union, deployed in dozens of conflicts around the globe for over 50 years; the invention of nonviolent struggle as a substitute for war, beginning with Gandhi, carried on by King, perfected in the struggles to overthrow the East European Communist Empire, Marcos in the Philippines, and Mubarak in Egypt and elsewhere (even used successfully against the Nazis); the invention of new techniques of conflict resolution known as non-adversarial bargaining, mutual gains bargaining, or win-win; the development of peace research and peace education including the rapid spread of peace research institutions and projects and peace education in hundreds of colleges and universities around the world; the peace conference movement, e.g., the Wisconsin Institute annual Student Conference, annual Fall Conference, the Peace and Justice Studies Association annual conference, the International Peace Research Association biennial conference, Pugwash annual peace conference, and many others.

In addition to these developments there is now a large body of peace literature – hundreds of books, journals, and thousands of articles – and the spread of democracy (it is a fact that democracies tend not to attack one another); the development of large regions of stable peace, especially in Scandinavia, U.S./Canada/Mexico, South America, and now Western Europe—where future war is either unthinkable or highly unlikely; the decline of racism and apartheid regimes and the end of political colonialism. We are, in fact, witnessing the end of empire. Empire is becoming an impossibility due to asymmetric warfare, nonviolent resistance, and astronomical costs that bankrupt the imperial state.

More parts of this peace revolution include the erosion of national sovereignty: nation states can no longer keep out immigrants, ideas, economic trends, disease organisms, intercontinental ballistic missiles, information, etc. Further advances include the development of the worldwide women's movement–education and rights for women have been spreading rapidly in the 20th century and, with notable exceptions, women tend to be more concerned with the well-being of families and the earth than are men. Educating girls is the single most important thing we can do to ensure sound

---

3. http://mettacenter.org/about/mission/

economic development. Further components of the revolution are the rise of the global environmental sustainability movement aimed at slowing and ending excessive consumption of resources and oil that create shortages, poverty, and pollution and exacerbate conflicts; the spread of peace-oriented forms of religion (the Christianity of Thomas Merton and Jim Wallis, the Episcopal Peace Fellowship, the Buddhism of the Dalai Lama, the Jewish Peace Fellowship, the Muslim Peace Fellowship and the Muslim Voice for Peace); and the rise of international civil society from a handful of INGOs in 1900 to tens of thousands today, creating a new, nongovernmental, citizen-based world system of communication and interaction for peace, justice, environmental preservation, sustainable economic development, human rights, disease control, literacy, and clean water; the rapid growth in the 20th century of an international law regime controlling war, including the Geneva Conventions, the treaties banning land mines and the use of child soldiers, atmospheric testing of nuclear weapons, placing nuclear weapons on the sea bed, etc.; the rise of the human rights movement, unprecedented before 1948 (Universal Declaration of Human Rights), once totally ignored, now an international norm whose violation is an outrage in most countries and brings immediate response from states and NGOs.

Nor is this all. The peace revolution includes the rise of the global conference movement such as the Earth Summit in 1992 in Rio, attended by 100 heads of state, 10,000 journalists, and 30,000 citizens. Since then global conferences on economic development, women, peace, global warming, and other topics have been held, creating a new forum for people from all over the world to come together to confront problems and create cooperative solutions; the further evolution of a system of diplomacy with well-established norms of diplomatic immunity, 3rd party good offices, permanent missions—all designed to allow states to communicate even in conflict situations; and the development of global interactive communication via the World Wide Web and cell phones means that ideas about democracy, peace, environment, and human rights spread almost instantly. The peace revolution also includes the appearance of peace journalism as writers and editors have become more thoughtful and critical of war propaganda and more attuned to the sufferings that war causes. Perhaps most important are shifting attitudes about war, a sharp decline in this century of the old attitude that war is a glorious and noble enterprise. At best, people think it is a dirty, violent necessity. A special part of this new story is spreading information about the record of successful nonviolent methods of peace and justice making.[4] The emergence of this embryonic global peace system is part of the larger development of a culture of peace.

Wherever people gather for selfless ends, there is vast augmentation of their individual capacities. Something wonderful, something momentous happens. An irresistible force begins to move, which, though we may not see it, is going to change our world.

Eknath Easwaraen (Spiritual Leader)

4. These trends are presented in depth in the study guide "The Evolution of a Global Peace System"and the short documentary provided by the War Prevention Initiative at http://warpreventioninitiative.org/?page_id=2674 .

Debunking Old Myths about War

Modern societies are often guided by a set of beliefs about conflict that are at best unquestioned myths. These need to be widely challenged. They are:

Myth: It is impossible to eliminate war.

Fact: to say this is to submit fatalistically to determinism, to believe that we humans do not make our history but are the helpless victims of forces beyond our control, that we have no free will. In fact, it was once said that it was impossible to abolish legalized slavery, dueling, blood feuds and other institutions that were deeply embedded in societies of their time, practices that are now, if not fully in the dustbin of history, universally understood to be eliminable. War is a social invention, not a permanent feature of human existence. It is a choice, not something imposed by a law of nature.

Myth: War is in our genes.

Fact: if this were true, all societies would be making war all of the time, which we know is not the case. During the most recent 6,000 years, war has been sporadic and some societies have not known war.[5] Some have known it and then abandoned it. Quite a few nations have chosen to have no military.[6] War is a social, not a biological event.

Myth: War is "natural."

Fact: it is very difficult to get people to kill in warfare. A great deal of psychological conditioning is required even to get them to fire their guns and very often they are traumatized by the experience and suffer post-traumatic stress disorder. Many veterans of combat end up chemically dependent and many commit suicide, unable to live with what they have done. Mass killing is not a part of our nature—quite the opposite is true.

Myth: We have always had war.

Fact: war is an invention of the last five percent of human existence. Archeology finds little evidence of weapons or war-gods or dominator societies before 4,000 b.C.E.

5. Social scientists have convincingly described at least 25 societies around the world in which there is very little internal violence or external warfare. See more at http://peacefulsocieties.org/

6. The most prominent example of Costa Rica's path of demilitarization is featured in the 2016 documentary *A Bold Peace* (http://aboldpeace.com/)

Myth: War is inevitable because of crises beyond our control like resource scarcity, environmental crises, over-population, etc.

Fact: humans are capable of rational behavior. War is always a choice and other choices are always possible if humans use their genetically endowed imaginations and inventiveness. Nonviolent resistance is always a choice, as are negotiation, economic sanctions, and many other responses to aggression.

Myth: We are a sovereign nation.

Fact: sovereignty rests on the belief that a people can draw a line around themselves and keep out anything they do not want to enter their nation, by war as a last resort. In fact, borders are now wholly permeable. One cannot keep out intercontinental ballistic missiles, ideas and information, disease organisms, refugees and migrants, economic influences, new technologies, the effects of climate shift, cyber-attacks, and cultural artifacts such as films and musical trends. Furthermore, most countries are not at all homogeneous but have highly mixed populations.

Myth: We go to war to ensure our defense.

Fact: "defense" is different from "offense." Defense means to protect one's borders from incursion as opposed to aggression, which is to cross another nation's borders to attack them. Establishing military bases around the world is offensive and it is counterproductive, stimulating hostility and threats rather than eliminating them. It makes us less secure. A defensive military posture would consist only of a coast guard, border patrol, anti-aircraft weapons, and other forces able to repel attack. Current "defense spending" by the u.S. Is almost wholly for projecting military power worldwide: offense, not defense.

> But if the term has any meaning, it cannot be stretched to cover offensive war making or aggressive militarism. If 'defense' is to mean something other than 'offense,' then attacking another nation 'so that they can't attack us first' or 'to send a message' or to 'punish' a crime is not defensive and not necessary.

David Swanson (Author, Activist)

> We are at a stage in human history where we can say with confidence that we know better and more effective alternatives to war and violence.
> (Patrick Hiller, Peace Scientist)

Myth: Some wars are "good" wars; for example, World War II.

Fact: it is true that cruel regimes were destroyed in world war ii, but to assert this is to use a curious definition of "good." World war ii resulted in overwhelming destruction of cities and all their cultural treasures, in an economic loss of unprecedented proportions, in massive environmental pollution, and (not least) the deaths of 100 million people, the maiming and dislocation of millions of others, the birth of two new superpowers, and the unleashing of the age of nuclear terror. And both sides of world war ii had the option in the preceding years and decades, of taking steps that would have avoided warfare.

Myth: the "Just War Doctrine"

Fact: the doctrine of just war, i.E., That a war is justified in spite of the general injunction to prefer peace, comes out of a fourth century c.E. Rejection of the traditional christian practice of pacifism. This doctrine stated that in order to go to war many criteria had to be satisfied, including that the war had to be fought with proportionate means (the evil of the destruction could not outweigh the evil of not going to war), and that civilians were never to be attacked.[7] The purposeful slaughter of civilians by mass aerial bombardment and the onset of the colossal deadliness of nuclear weapons make world war ii an unjust war. In fact, given modern weapons (even so-called "smart bombs") it is impossible to wage war without killing innocent children, women, old men, and other non-combatants. Calling this evil "collateral damage" does not make an exception for it — it simply describes it with a deceitful euphemism. Finally, the now-proven alternative of nonviolent defense provides a resistance response to tyranny and invasion that satisfies all the criteria of just war without destroying millions of lives and is a response that returns civilization to original "christian" values. No war can satisfy the conditions of absolute last resort. In the wars of the last twenty years, the most important motive has been to control

---

7. In the Spring of 2015, the Vatican hosted the conference "Nonviolence and Just Peace: Contributing to the Catholic Understanding of and Commitment to Nonviolence". 80 participants concluded that the just war doctrine should be rejected as a viable or productive Catholic tradition. See the insightful article *Did the Vatican just throw out its just war doctrine* by Erica Chenoweth at https://politicalviolenceataglance.org/2016/04/19/did-the-vatican-just-throw-out-its-just-war-doctrine/

the flow of oil out of the middle east, and, as we have seen, the so-called "war on terror" has only created more terrorists. However, a permanent state of war does benefit a small elite of war manufacturers and suppliers and serves as an excuse to restrict civil liberties.

Myth: War and war preparation bring peace and stability.
Fact: the ancient romans said, "if you want peace, prepare for war." What they got was war after war until it destroyed them. What the romans considered "peace" was dictating terms to the helpless conquered, much as occurred after world war i at which time an observer said that this was not a peace but a truce that would last only twenty years, which turned out to be the case. Making war creates resentment, new enemies, distrust, and further wars. Preparation for war makes other nations feel they must also prepare and so a vicious circle is created which perpetuates the war system.

Myth: War makes us safe. War may be unjust and bloody but in the end it makes us safe. Corollary: "The price of freedom is blood."
Fact: war makes everyone less safe. The losers lose, the winners lose, and all the survivors lose. In fact, no one wins a modern war. Many are killed on both sides. If by chance the "winners" fight the war in the losers' land, the winners nevertheless have many killed, spend treasure that could have been used to benefit their own citizens, and pollute the earth through greenhouse gas emissions and the release of toxins. The "victorious war" paves the way for future arms races and instability, leading eventually to the next war. War simply doesn't work.

Myth: War is necessary to kill the terrorists.
Fact: war mythology tells us that "our" wars (whoever "we" are) kill evil people who need to be killed to protect us and our freedoms. In fact, while some "terrorists" are killed, recent wars waged by wealthy nations are one-sided slaughters of innocents and ordinary residents and end up creating more terrorists while poisoning the natural environment. Rather than choosing a violent response to terrorism or invasion, which are just symptoms of a conflict problem, it is more sensible to

Photo: Pancho Ramos

look for the causes of the disease which has led to the conflict. In particular, it is more effective to learn about the history and what part your nation might have played in creating the conflict and the hostility so that the problem can be dealt with at its root. Otherwise, a violent response just perpetuates and escalates the conflict.

Myth: War is good for the economy and benefits the war makers.

Fact: war and war preparation weaken an economy. Some people argue that it was world war ii that got the west or the united states out of the great depression. In fact, it was government deficit spending that restarted the economy. The spending just happened to be on war production, things that when used nevertheless destroyed economic value. The spending could have gone for economic goods that improved the standard of living. It is well documented that a dollar spent on education and health care produces more jobs than the same dollar spent in the war industry, and a dollar spent on use value (rather than bombs) such as rebuilding roads or establishing green energy provides for the common good. Dollars spent to maintain the flow of oil end up polluting not only where it is eventually burned, but the oil used to power the military machine (in the u.S., 340,000 Barrels a day) also leads to a degrading of the environment. While war spending benefits a small number of war profiteers, peace is good for everyone and for the natural environment.

Planetary Citizenship: One People, One Planet, One Peace

Humans constitute a single species, Homo sapiens. While we have developed a marvelous diversity of ethnic, religious, economic, and political systems which enrich our common life, we are in fact one people living on a very fragile planet. The biosphere which supports our lives and our civilizations is extremely thin, like the skin of an apple. Within it is everything we all need to stay alive and well. We all share in one atmosphere, one great ocean, one global climate, one single source of fresh water endlessly cycled around the earth, one great biodiversity. These constitute the biophysical commons on which civilization rests. It is gravely threatened by our industrial way of life, and our common task is to preserve it from destruction if we wish to live on.

Today the single most important responsibility of national governments and governing agreements at the international level is the protection of the commons. We need to think first of the health of the global commons and only second in terms of national interest, for the latter is now totally dependent on the former. A perfect storm of

global environmental disasters is already underway including unprecedented rates of extinction, a depletion of global fisheries, an unprecedented soil erosion crisis, massive deforestation, and accelerating and making these worse, a climate disaster in the making. We face a planetary emergency.

The commons also includes the social commons which is the condition of just peace. All must be safe if any are to be safe. The safety of any must guarantee the safety of all. A just peace is a society in which there is no fear of violent attack (war or civil war), of exploitation of one group by another, no political tyranny, where everyone's basic needs are met, and where all have the right to participate in the decisions that impact them. Just as a healthy biophysical commons requires biological diversity, a healthy social commons requires social diversity.

Protecting the commons is best achieved by voluntary consensus so that it is a self-organizing process from below, a function of shared values and mutual respect that arise out of a sense of responsibility for the planet's well-being. When consensus is not available, when some individuals, corporations, or nations do not care about the common good, when they want to make war or degrade the environment for gain, then government is needed to protect the commons and that means laws, courts, and the police power necessary to enforce them.

We have reached a stage in human and evolutionary history where the protection of the commons is necessary not only to the good life for humanity, but to our very survival. This means new ideas, especially the realization that we are a single planetary community. It also includes creating new associations, new forms of democratic governance and new agreements between nations to protect the commons.

War not only distracts us from this vital task, but it adds to the destruction. We will never end conflict on the planet, but conflict does not have to lead to war. We are a highly intelligent species who have already developed nonviolent methods of conflict resolution which can, and in some cases are, taking the place of violent means. We need to scale these up until we provide for common security, a world where all the children are safe and healthy, free from fear, want, and persecution, a successful human civilization resting on a healthy biosphere. One people, one planet, one peace is the essence of the new story we need to tell. It is the next stage in the progress of civilization. In order to grow and spread the culture of peace we need to reinforce several already ongoing trends.

Spreading and Funding Peace Education and Peace Research

For millennia we educated ourselves about war, focusing our best minds on how to win it. Just as narrow-minded historians had insisted there was no such thing as Black history or women's history, so too they argued there was no such thing as the history of peace. Humanity had failed to focus on peace until the new fields of peace research and peace education developed in the wake of the catastrophe that was World War II and accelerated in the 1980s after the world came close to nuclear annihilation. In the years since, there has been a vast increase in information about the conditions of peace.

Peace Science has emerged as an academic discipline now offered worldwide by more than 450 university programs. A myriad of peer-reviewed academic journals, textbooks, and conferences address both the theoretical and practical developments in the peacebuilding arena, as do peace research institutions like the Stockholm International Peace Research Institute or the Peace Research Institute Oslo, and professional associations like the International Peace Research Association and its regional affiliates in Africa, Asia, Europe, Latin America, and North America.

Lastly the Global Peace Index, now going into its 10th year, is probably the most renowned research-based measure of peacefulness or lack thereof. The point is, Peace Science is real and here to stay. (Give Peace Science a Chance in Diplomatic Courier)[8]

The United States Institute of Peace was established by Congress in 1984 as an independent, federally-funded national security institution devoted to the nonviolent prevention and mitigation of deadly conflict abroad.[9] It sponsors events, provides education and training and publications including a Peacemaker's Tool Kit. Unfortunately, the U.S. Institute of Peace has never been known to oppose U.S. wars. But all these institutions are substantial steps in the direction of spreading understanding of peaceful alternatives.

These organizations are a small sample of the institutions and individuals working on peace research. We have learned a great deal about how to create and maintain peace in the last fifty years. We are at a stage in human history where we can say with confidence that we know better and more effective alternatives to war and violence. Much of their work has provided for the development and growth of peace education.

Peace Education now embraces all levels of formal education from kindergarten through doctoral studies. The Global Campaign for Peace Education seeks to build awareness and political support for the introduction of peace education, including non-formal education, in all schools throughout the world and promote the education of all teachers to teach for peace.[10] Hundreds of college campuses provide majors, minors and certificate programs in peace education. At the university level the Peace and Justice Studies Association gathers researchers, teachers and peace activists for conferences and publishes a journal, The Peace Chronicle, and provides a resource base. Curricula and courses have multiplied and are taught as age-specific instruction at all levels. In addition a whole new field of literature has developed including hundreds of books, articles, videos and films about peace now available to the general public.

Cultivating Peace Journalism

How is the world ruled and how do wars start? Diplomats tell lies to journalists and then believe what they read.

Karl Kraus (Poet, Playwright)

The "warist" bias we commonly see in the teaching of history also infects mainstream journalism. Too many reporters, columnists, and news anchors are stuck in the old story that war is inevitable and that it brings peace. Moreover:

...in the media the "expertise" related to war and peace provided by members of the intelligentsia is very one-sided. Many of these eloquent individuals have achieved their legitimacy through academic credentials, military authority, or recognition as political commentators. Their facts, opinions, and advice on matters of war and peace shape the dominant discourse and mostly serve to uphold the status quo of a war system. (Give Peace Science a Chance in Diplomatic Courier)[11]

---

8. See the full article by Patrick Hiller in the Diplomatic Courier at http://www.diplomaticourier.com/2016/07/05/give-peace-science-chance/

9. http://www.usip.org/

10. The Global Campaign for Peace Education was founded at the Hague Appeal for Peace Conference in 1999. See more at: http://www.peace-ed-campaign.org

11. See the full article by Patrick Hiller in the Diplomatic Courier at http://www.diplomaticourier.com/2016/07/05/give-peace-science-chance/

There are, however, new initiatives in "peace journalism," a movement conceived by peace scholar Johan Galtung. In peace journalism, editors and writers give the reader a chance to consider nonviolent responses to conflict rather than the usual knee-jerk reaction of counter violence.[12] Peace Journalism focuses on the structural and cultural causes of violence and its impacts on actual people (rather than the abstract analysis of States), and frames conflicts in terms of their real complexity in contrast to war journalism's simple "good guys versus bad guys." It also seeks to publicize peace initiatives commonly ignored by the mainstream press. The Center for Global Peace Journalism publishes The Peace Journalist Magazine and offers 10 characteristics of "PJ":

> *1. PJ is proactive, examining the causes of conflict, and looking for ways to encourage dialogue before violence occurs. 2. PJ looks to unite parties, rather than divide them, and eschews oversimplified "us vs. them" and "good guy vs. bad guy" reporting. 3. Peace reporters reject official propaganda, and instead seek facts from all sources. 4. PJ is balanced, covering issues/suffering/peace proposals from all sides of a conflict. 5. PJ gives voice to the voiceless, instead of just reporting for and about elites and those in power. 6. Peace journalists provide depth and context, rather than just superficial and sensational "blow by blow" accounts of violence and conflict. 7. Peace journalists consider the consequences of their reporting. 8. Peace journalists carefully choose and analyze the words they use, understanding that carelessly selected words are often inflammatory. 9. Peace journalists thoughtfully select the images they use, understanding that they can misrepresent an event, exacerbate an already dire situation, and re-victimize those who have suffered. 10. Peace Journalists offer counter-narratives that debunk media-created or -perpetuated stereotypes, myths, and misperceptions.*

The following table based on Johan Galtung's work compares the Peace Journalism framework to the War/Violence Journalism framework:[13]

A notable example is Democracy Now!'s War and Peace Report. It provides the "audience with access to people and perspectives rarely heard in the U.S.corporate-sponsored media, including independent and international journalists, ordinary people from around the world who are directly affected by U.S. foreign policy, grassroots leaders and peace activists, artists, academics and independent analysts".[14]

Another example is PeaceVoice, a project of the Oregon Peace Institute.[15] PeaceVoice welcomes submission of op-eds that take a "new story" approach to international conflict and then distributes them to newspapers and blogs around the United States. Taking advantage of the internet, there are many blogs that also distribute the new paradigm thinking including Waging Nonviolence, the Transcend Media Service, New Clear Vision, Peace Action Blog, Waging Peace Blog, Bloggers for Peace and many other sites on the World Wide Web.

With growing recognition of Peace Journalism, viable alternatives to the common destructive responses in the war system will be made available to the many publics. Once those alternatives come to light, it has been proven that there will be a decline in public support for war.[16]

---

12. It is a growing movement, according to the website www.peacejournalism.org

13. Galtung's table re-created in Lynch, Jake, and Annabel McGoldrick. 2007. "Peace Journalism." *In Handbook of Peace and Conflict Studies*, edited by Charles Webel and Johan Galtung, 248–64. London; New York: Routledge.

14. See www.democracynow.org

15. See www.peacevoice.info

16. See Peace Science Digest analysis Proven Decline in Public Support for War When the Alternatives Come to Light at http://communication.warpreventioninitiative.org/?p=227

Peace/Journalism	War/Violence Journalism
I. Peace/conflict oriented	I. War/violence-oriented
Explore conflict formation, x parties, y goals, z issues General 'win, win' orientation Open space, open time; causes and outcomes anywhere, also in history/culture Making conflicts transparent Giving voice to all parties; empathy, understanding See conflict/war as problem, focus on conflict creativity Humanization of all sides Proactive: prevention before any violence/war occurs	Focus on conflict arena, 2 parties, 1 goal (win), war General zero-sum orientation Closed space, closed time; causes and exits in arena, who threw the first stone Making wars opaque/secret 'Us-them' journalism, propaganda, voice, for 'us' See 'them' as the problem, focus on who prevails in war Dehumanization of 'them' Reactive: waiting for violence before reporting Focus on invisible effects of violence (trauma and glory, damage to structure/culture
II. Truth-oriented	II. Propaganda-oriented
Expose untruths on all sides / uncover all cover-ups	Expose 'their' untruths / help 'our' cover-ups/lies
III. People-oriented	III. Elite-oriented
Focus on suffering all over; on women, the Aged, children, giving voice to voiceless Give name to all evil-doers Focus on people as peacemakers	Focus on 'our' suffering; on able-bodied elite males, being their mouth-piece Give name to their evil-doers Focus on elite peacemakers
IV. Solution-oriented	IV. Victory-oriented
Peace = nonviolence + creativity Highlight peace initiatives, also to prevent more war Focus on structure, culture, the peaceful society Aftermath: resolution, reconstruction, reconciliation	Peace = victory + ceasefire Conceal peace initiative, before victory is at hand Focus on treaty, institution, the controlled society Leaving for another war, return if the old flares up again

Peace research, education, journalism and blogging are part of the newly developing culture of peace, as are recent developments in religion.

Encouraging the Work of Peaceful Religious Initiatives

Peace has been a religious concern for much of history. At the same time we have to recognize that religion has been used to justify violence and wars. In the contemporary world, religious extremism often ignites violence. We must not fall into the thought-trap of allowing religious interpretation and misinterpretation and false labeling to lead us to black-and-white assumptions about religious violence.

Just think about the following examples. In his human approach to world peace the Buddhist spiritual leader Dalai Lama advocates loving kindness. In the build-up to military intervention in Syria, Pope Francis made a compelling appeal for seeking a peaceful resolution. During the 2011 Egyptian Revolution Nevin Zaki captured and tweeted the powerful image of Christians joining hands in a circle to protect a Muslim group of protesters as they prayed. These are just a few snapshots of a larger trend of growing advocacy of peace messages in all major religions.

Throughout the history of nonviolence we have seen the importance of faith communities, recognizing that many nonviolent leaders were/are people of strong religious and moral faith. Just consider this simple quote by Catholic writer and peace advocate Thomas Merton:

> War is the kingdom of Satan. Peace is the kingdom of God.

Regardless of one's faith tradition, rejection of institutional religion, spiritual direction or complete atheism, the work by peaceful religious initiatives is encouraging and should be further encouraged.[17]

The followers of every religion can cite sources from scripture that justify violence, but all of the world's religions also contain scriptural teachings that advocate peaceful relationships among all people. The former must be debunked in favor of the latter. The "golden rule" is found in one form or another in them all, as in the scriptures below, as well as in the ethics of most atheists.

> *Christianity: Whatever you wish that men would do to you, do so to them. Matthew 7.12*

> *Judaism: What is hateful to you, do not do to your neighbor. Talmud, Shabbat 31a*

> *Islam: Not one of you is a believer until he loves for his brother what he loves for himself. Forty Hadith of an-Nawawi 13*

> *Hinduism: One should not behave towards others in a way which is disagreeable to oneself. This is the essence of morality. Mahabharata, Anusasana Parva 113.8*

> *Buddhism: Comparing oneself to others in such terms as "Just as I am so are they, just as they are so am I," he should neither kill nor cause others to kill. Sutta Nipata 705*

17. Two historically antagonistic perspectives are: (1) religion is the only way to peace; (2) religion is inherently conflictual. A more flexible perspective is peace through religion where the role of religious thinking in the public sphere and the potential contributions of religion are examined

African Traditional: One going to take a pointed stick to pinch a baby bird should first try it on himself to feel how it hurts. Yoruba Proverb (Nigeria)

Confucianism: Do not do to others what you do not want them to do to you." Analects 15.23

Many religions host organizations for peace such as the Episcopal Peace Fellowship, Pax Christi, the Jewish Voice for Peace, Muslims For Peace, the Buddhist Peace Fellowship, Yakjah (a Hindu peace organization working in the Kashmir), etc. Many interfaith peace organizations are also thriving from the oldest, the Fellowship of Reconciliation, United Religions Initiative, and Religions for Peace USA to numerous recent foundings such as Multi-faith Voices for Peace and Justice, founded in 2003. The World Council of Churches is heading up a campaign to abolish nuclear weapons.

The outlined perspectives on religions and peace hopefully leave the more antagonistic ones behind - namely that religion is the only way to peace or that religion is inherently conflictual. It is not a question of "peace through religion" or "peace without religion". It is about whether individuals or groups chose to adopt faith-based identities in their work toward a World Beyond War or not.

ACCELERATING THE TRANSITION TO AN ALTERNATIVE SECURITY SYSTEM

World Beyond War intends to accelerate the movement toward ending war and establishing a peace system in two ways: massive education, and nonviolent action to dismantle the war machine.

If we want war to end, we are going to have to work to end it. It requires activism, structural change and a shift in consciousness. Even when recognizing the long-term historical trends of declining warfare – by no means an uncontroversial claim – it won't continue doing so without work. In fact, the 2016 Global Peace Index has shown that the world has become less peaceful. And as long as there is any war, there is a significant danger of widespread war. Wars are notoriously hard to control once begun. With nuclear weapons in the world (and with nuclear plants as potential targets), any war-making carries a risk of apocalypse. War-making and war preparations are destroying our natural environment and diverting resources from a possible rescue effort that would preserve a habitable climate. As a matter of survival, war and preparations for war must be completely abolished, and abolished quickly, by replacing the war system with a peace system.

To accomplish this, we will need a peace movement that differs from past movements that have been against each successive war or against each offensive weapon. We cannot fail to oppose wars, but we must also oppose the entire institution and work toward replacing it.

World Beyond War intends to work globally. While begun in the United States, World Beyond War has worked to include individuals and organizations from around the globe in its decision making. Thousands of people in 134 countries have thus far signed the pledge on the WorldBeyondWar.org website to work for the elimination of all war.

War does not have a single source, but it does have a largest one. Ending war-making by the United States and its allies would go a very long way toward ending war globally. For those living in the United States, at least, one key place to start ending war is within the U.S. government. This can be worked on together with people affected by U.S. wars and those living near U.S. military bases around the world, which is a fairly large percentage of the people on earth.

Ending U.S. militarism wouldn't eliminate war globally, but it would eliminate the pressure that is driving several other nations to increase their military spending. It would deprive NATO of its leading advocate for and greatest participant in wars. It would cut off the largest supply of weapons to Western Asia (a.k.a. the Middle East) and other regions. It would remove the major barrier to reconciliation and reunification of Korea. It would create U.S. willingness to support arms treaties, join the International Criminal Court, and allow the United Nations to move in the direction of its stated purpose of eliminating war. It would create a world free of nations

threatening first-use of nukes, and a world in which nuclear disarmament might proceed more rapidly. Gone would be the last major nation using cluster bombs or refusing to ban landmines. If the United States kicked the war habit, war itself would suffer a major and possibly fatal set-back.

A focus on U.S. war preparations cannot work as well without similar efforts everywhere. Numerous nations are investing, and even increasing their investments, in war. All militarism must be opposed. And victories for a peace system tend to spread by example. When the British Parliament opposed attacking Syria in 2013 it helped block that U.S. proposal. When 31 nations committed in Havana, Cuba, in January 2014 to never making use of war, those voices were heard in other nations of the world.[1]

Global solidarity in educational efforts constitutes an important part of the education itself. Student and cultural exchanges between the West and nations on the Pentagon's likely target list (Syria, Iran, North Korea, China, Russia, etc.) will go a long way toward building resistance toward those potential future wars. Similar exchanges between nations investing in war and nations that have ceased to do so, or which do so at a greatly reduced scale, can be of great value as well.[2]

Building a global movement for stronger and more democratic global structures of peace will also require educational efforts that do not stop at national borders.

Partial steps toward replacing the war system will be pursued, but they will be understood as and discussed as just that: partial steps on the way toward creating a peace system. Such steps may include banning weaponized drones or closing particular bases or eliminating nuclear weapons or closing the School of the Americas, defunding military advertising campaigns, restoring war powers to the legislative branch, cutting off weapons sales to dictatorships, etc.

Finding the strength in numbers to do these things is part of the purpose of the collection of signatures on the simple Pledge Statement.[3] World Beyond War hopes to facilitate the forming of a broader coalition suited to the task. This will mean bringing together all those sectors that rightfully ought to be opposing the military industrial complex: moralists, ethicists, preachers of morality and ethics, religious community, doctors, psychologists, and protectors of human health, economists, labor unions, workers, civil libertarians, advocates for democratic reforms, journalists, historians, promoters of transparency in public decision-making, internationalists, those hoping to travel and be liked abroad, environmentalists, and proponents of everything worthwhile on which war dollars could be spent instead: education, housing, arts, science, etc. That's a pretty big group.

Many activist organizations want to stay focused in their niches. Many are reluctant to risk being called unpatriotic. Some are tied up in profits from military contracts. World Beyond War will work around these barriers. This will involve asking civil libertarians to view war as the root cause of the symptoms they treat, and asking environmentalists to view war as at least one of the major root problems — and its elimination as a possible solution.

---

1. See more on the Community of Latin American and Caribbean states at: http://www.nti.org/treaties-and-regimes/community-latin-american-and-caribbean-states-celac/

2. Peace Scientist Patrick Hiller found in his research that experiences abroad of U.S. citizens led them to better recognize U.S. privilege and perception around the world, to understand how perceived enemies are dehumanized in the U.S. main narrative, to see 'the other' in a positive way, to reduce prejudices and stereotypes, and to create empathy.

3. The Pledge can be found and signed at: http://worldbeyondwar.org/

Green energy has far greater potential to handle our energy needs (and wants) than is commonly supposed, because the massive transfer of money that would be possible with the abolition of war isn't usually considered. Human needs across the board can be better met than we usually imagine, because we don't usually consider withdrawing $2 trillion a year globally from the world's deadliest criminal enterprise.

Toward these ends, WBW will be working to organize a bigger coalition ready and trained to engage in nonviolent direct action, creatively, generously, and fearlessly.

Educating the Many and the Decision and Opinion Makers

Using a bi-level approach and working with other citizen based organizations, World Beyond War will launch a world-wide campaign to educate the masses of people that war is a failed social institution that can be abolished to the great benefit of all. Books, print media articles, speaker's bureaus, radio and television appearances, electronic media, conferences, etc., will be employed to spread the word about the myths and institutions that perpetuate war. The aim is to create a planetary consciousness and a demand for a just peace without undermining in any way the benefits of unique cultures and political systems.

World Beyond War has begun and will continue to support and promote good work in this direction by other organizations, including many organizations that have signed the pledge at WorldBeyondWar.org. Already distant connections have been made among organizations in various parts of the world that have proved mutually beneficial. World Beyond War will combine its own initiatives with this sort of assistance for others' in an effort to create greater cooperation and greater coherence around the idea of a movement to end all war. The result of educational efforts favored by World Beyond War will be a world in which talk of a "good war" will sound no more possible than a "benevolent rape" or "philanthropic slavery" or "virtuous child abuse."

World Beyond War seeks to create a moral movement against an institution that should be viewed as tantamount to mass-murder, even when that mass-murder is accompanied by flags or music or assertions of authority and promotion of irrational fear. World Beyond War advocates against the practice of opposing a particular war on the grounds that it isn't being run well or isn't as proper as some other war. World Beyond War seeks to strengthen its moral argument by taking the focus of peace activism partially away from the harm wars do to the aggressors, in order to fully acknowledge and appreciate the suffering of all.

In the film The Ultimate Wish: Ending the Nuclear Age we see a survivor of Nagasaki meeting a survivor of Auschwitz. It is hard in watching them meeting and speaking together to remember or care which nation committed which horror. A peace culture will see all war with that same clarity. War is an abomination not because of who commits it but because of what it is.

World Beyond War intends to make war abolition the sort of cause that slavery abolition was and to hold up resisters, conscientious objectors, peace advocates, diplomats, whistleblowers, journalists, and activists as our heroes — in fact, to develop alternative avenues for heroism and glory, including nonviolent activism, and including serving as peace workers and human shields in places of conflict.

World Beyond War will not promote the idea that "peace is patriotic," but rather that thinking in terms of world citizenship is helpful in the cause of peace. WBW will work to remove nationalism, xenophobia, racism, religious bigotry, and exceptionalism from popular thinking.

Central projects in World Beyond War's early efforts will be the provision of useful information through the WorldBeyondWar.org website, and the collection of a large number of individual and organizational signatures on the pledge posted there. The website is constantly being updated with maps, charts, graphics, arguments, talking points, and videos to help people make the case, to themselves and others, that wars can/should/must be abolished. Each section of the website includes lists of relevant books, and one such list is in the Appendix to this document.

The WBW Pledge Statement reads as follows:

> *I understand that wars and militarism make us less safe rather than protect us, that they kill, injure and traumatize adults, children and infants, severely damage the natural environment, erode civil liberties, and drain our economies, siphoning resources from life-affirming activities. I commit to engage in and support nonviolent efforts to end all war and preparations for war and to create a sustainable and just peace.*

World Beyond War is collecting signatures on this statement on paper at events and adding them to the website, as well as inviting people to add their names online. If a large number of those who would be willing to sign this statement can be reached and asked to do so, that fact will potentially be persuasive news to others. The same goes for the inclusion of signatures by well-known figures. The collection of signatures is a tool for advocacy in another way as well; those signers who choose to join a World Beyond War email list can later be contacted to help advance a project initiated in their part of the world.

Expanding the reach of the Pledge Statement, signers are asked to make use of WBW tools to contact others, share information online, write letters to editors, lobby governments and other bodies, and organize small gatherings. Resources to facilitate all kinds of outreach are provided at WorldBeyondWar.org.

Beyond its central projects, WBW will be participating in and promoting useful projects begun by other groups and testing out new specific initiatives of its own.

One area that WBW hopes to work on is the creation of truth and reconciliation commissions, and greater appreciation of their work. Lobbying for the establishment of an International Truth and Reconciliation Commission or Court is a possible area of focus as well.

Other areas in which World Beyond War may put some effort, beyond its central project of advancing the idea of ending all war, include: disarmament; conversion to peaceful industries; asking new nations to join and current Parties to abide by the Kellogg-Briand Pact; lobbying for reforms of the United Nations; lobbying governments and other bodies for various initiatives, including a Global Marshall Plan or parts thereof; and countering recruitment efforts while strengthening the rights of conscientious objectors.

Nonviolent Direct Action Campaigns

World Beyond War believes that little is more important than advancing common understanding of nonviolence as an alternative form of conflict to violence, and ending the habit of thinking that one can ever be faced with only the choices of engaging in violence or doing nothing.

In addition to its education campaign, World Beyond War will work with other organizations to launch nonviolent, Gandhian-style protests and nonviolent direct action

campaigns against the war machine in order to disrupt it and to demonstrate the strength of the popular desire to end war. The goal of this campaign will be to compel the political decision makers and those who make money from the killing machine to come to the table for talks on ending war and replacing it with a more effective alternative security system. World Beyond War has endorsed and worked with Campaign Nonviolence, a long-term movement for a culture of peace and nonviolence free from war, poverty, racism, environmental destruction and the epidemic of violence.[4] The campaign aims to mainstream nonviolent direct action and connect the dots war, poverty and climate change.

This nonviolent effort will benefit from the education campaign, but will also in its turn serve an educational purpose. Huge public campaigns/movements have a way of bringing people's attention to questions they have not been focused on.

The Alternative Global Security System Concept - a Movement Building Tool[5]

What we outlined here as the Alternative Global Security System is not only a concept, but it contains many elements of a peace and security infrastructure creating an unprecedented social space and opportunities for a re-energized movement to abolish war.

Communication

Communicating on war and peace issues is accompanied by multiple symbols and symbolism. Peace, especially in western peace movements, has several recurring symbolic elements: the peace sign, doves, olive branches, people holding hands, and variations of the globe. While generally non-contentious, they fail to communicate tangible meanings of peace. Especially when juxtaposing war and peace, the images and symbolism depicting the destructive consequences of war are often accompanied by the traditional peace symbolism.

1. AGSS offers an opportunity to provide humans with a new vocabulary and a vision of realistic alternatives to war and paths toward common security.

2. AGSS as a concept in itself is a powerful alternative narrative consisting of multiple narratives across nations and cultures.

3. AGSS offers a broad framework for communicating on nonviolent constructive conflict transformation approaches

4. AGSS is broad and can reach more bystanders by tapping into ongoing hot-topics (e.g. climate change) or the recurring events like gun violence or death penalty.

Palatable to mainstream audiences

Using common language and more importantly appealing to common values makes it more palatable to mainstream and is something that effective elites have been practicing for their purposes.

1. AGSS offers many opportunities to get involvement within the acceptable societal narrative.

2. Through the AGSS perspective anti-war activists can situate their work within

4. http://www.paceebene.org/programs/campaign-nonviolence/

5. This section is based on Patrick Hiller's paper and presentation The Global Peace System – an unprecedented infrastructure of peace for re-energized movements to abolish war. It was presented at the 2014 conference of the International Peace Research Association Conference in Istanbul, Turkey.

trends that address hunger, poverty, racism, the economy, climate change, and several other factors.

3. A specific mention should be given to the role of peace research and peace education. We now can talk about "peace science". 450 undergraduate and graduate peace and conflict studies programs and K-12 peace education demonstrate that the discipline no longer is at the margins.

When framing, rhetoric and goals are more acceptable in the mainstream, some movement organizers might perceive a cooptation of the movement, yet we hope that the entry of the movement ideas into the mainstream – or even the shifting of mainstream values - are signs of movement success. It will be up to us to determine the path.

Broader network

It is obvious that no movement can act in isolation of its social context and in isolation of other movements should it be successful.

AGSS offers a mental and practical framework to connect the disconnected. While the recognition of the interrelatedness of the different elements is not really new, the practical implementation is still lacking. Anti-war activism is the primary focus, but cross movement support and collaboration is now possible on a broad range of issues outlined in the AGSS framework.

Continued organizational identity

AGSS offers a unifying language where different social movement organizations can pertain to alliances without losing their organizational or movement identity. It is possible to identify an aspect of the work and specifically connect it to being part of an alternative global security system.

Synergy

Synergy can be achieved with the recognition of AGSS. As peace researcher Houston Wood points out, "peace and justice individuals and organizations across the world now form an emergent global peace consciousness that is different and more powerful than the sum of its dispersed parts". He adds that linked elements of the network will increase its range and density, opening even more space for growth. His projection is that the global peace network will grew even more powerful in the decades ahead.

Renewed hope

When people realize that AGSS exists, they will be inspired to act for a goal as large a world without war. Let us make this assumption a reality. The focus of WBW is clear – abolish the failed institution of war. Nevertheless, in building a re-energized anti-war movement we have a unique opportunity to enter into coalitions and alliances where partners recognize the potential of the AGSS, identify themselves and their work as part of the trends and create synergistic effects to strengthen the system. We have new opportunities for education, networking and action. Coalitions at this level can potentially create a counterbalance to the dominating war narrative through the active creation of an alternative story and reality. In thinking about a world beyond war and an alternative global security system we should refrain from imagining a nonviolent utopia. The institution and practice of war can be abolished. It is a socially constructed phenomenon which is overwhelming, yet on the decline. Peace then is an ongoing process of human evolution where constructive, nonviolent ways of conflict transformation are predominant.

7. CONCLUSION

War is always a choice and it is always a bad choice. It is a choice that always leads to more war. It is not mandated in our genes or our human nature. It is not the only possible response to conflicts. Nonviolent action and resistance is a better choice because it defuses and helps resolve conflict. But the choice for nonviolence must not wait until conflict erupts. It must be built into society: built into institutions for conflict forecasting, mediation, adjudication, and peacekeeping. It must be built into education in the form of knowledge, perceptions, beliefs and values—in short, a culture of peace. Societies consciously prepare far in advance for the war response and so perpetuate insecurity.

Some powerful groups benefit from war and violence. The vast majority of humans, however, will gain a lot from a world without war. The movement will work on strategies for outreach to a wide variety of constituencies globally. Such constituencies might include people in many parts of the world, key organizers, well-known leaders, peace groups, peace and justice groups, environmental groups, human rights groups, activist coalitions, lawyers, philosophers/ moralists/ethicists, doctors, psychologists, religious groups, economists, labor unions, diplomats, towns and cities and states or provinces or regions, nations, international organizations, the United Nations, civil liberties groups, media reform groups, business groups and leaders, billionaires, teachers groups, student groups, education reform groups, government reform groups, journalists, historians, women's groups, senior citizens, immigrant and refugee rights groups, libertarians, socialists, liberals, Democrats, Republicans, conservatives, veterans, student- and cultural-exchange groups, sister-cities groups, sports enthusiasts, and advocates for investment in children and health care and in human needs of every sort, as well as those working to oppose contributors to militarism in their societies, such as xenophobia, racism, machismo, extreme materialism, all forms of violence, lack of community, and war profiteering.

For peace to prevail, we must prepare equally far in advance for the better choice. If you want peace, prepare for peace.

> *Forget that this task of planet-saving is not possible in the time required. Don't be put off by people who know what is not possible. Do what needs to be done, and check to see if it was impossible only after you are done.*

Paul Hawken (Environmentalist, Author)

be inspired

- In less than two years, thousands of people from 135 countries have signed World Beyond War's pledge for peace.

- Demilitarization is underway. Costa Rica and 24 other countries have disbanded their militaries altogether.

- European nations, which had fought each other for over a thousand years, including the horrendous world wars of the twentieth century, now work collaboratively in the European Union.

- Former advocates of nuclear weapons, including former U.S. Senators and Secretaries of State and numerous retired, high-ranking military officers, have publicly rejected nuclear weapons and called for their abolition.

- There is a massive, worldwide movement to end the carbon economy and hence the wars over oil.

- Many thoughtful people and organizations around the world are calling for an end to the counter-productive "war on terror."

- At least one million organizations in the world are actively working toward peace, social justice, and environmental protection.

- Thirty-one Latin American and Caribbean nations created a zone of peace on January 29, 2014.

- In the last 100 years, we humans have created for the first time in history institutions and movements to control international violence: the UN, the World Court, the International Criminal Court; and treaties such as the Kellogg-Briand Pact, the Treaty to Ban Landmines, the Treaty to Ban Child Soldiers, and many others.

- A peace revolution is already underway.

APPENDIX

Resource Guide

Peace Almanac - http://worldbeyondwar.org/calendar/
Mapping Military Madness Update 2015 - http://worldbeyondwar.org/mapping-military-madness-2015-update/
Where Your Income Tax Money Really Goes- https://www.warresisters.org/resources/
pie-chart-flyers-where-your-income-tax-money-really-goes
Peace Science Digest - www.communication.warpreventioninitiative.org
Global Peace Index - http://www.visionofhumanity.org/

Books

Ackerman, Peter, and Jack DuVall, *A Force More Powerful: A Century of Nonviolent Conflict* (2000).

American Friends Service Committee, *Shared Security: Reimagining U.S. Foreign Policy.*
(https://afsc.org/sites/afsc.civicactions.net/files/documents/shared-security_web.pdf)

Amster, Randall, *Peace Ecology* (2014).

Bacevich, Andrew, *The new American militarism: how Americans are seduced by war* (2005).

Bacevich, Andrew, *Washington rules: America's path to permanent war* (2010).

Benjamin, Medea, & Evans, Jodie, *Stop the next war now: effective responses to violence and terrorism* (2005).

Boulding, Elise, and Randall Forsberg, *Abolishing War: Cultures and Institutions* (1998).

Boulding, Elise, *Cultures of Peace: The Hidden Side of History* (2000).

Boyle, Francis Anthony, *Defending Civil Resistance Under International Law* (1987).

Buchheit, Paul, *American Wars: Illusions and Realities* (2008).

Burrowes, Robert J. *The Strategy of Nonviolent Defense: A Gandhian Approach* (1996).

Cady, Duane L., *From Warism to Pacifism: A Moral Continuum* (2010).

Chappell, Paul, *The Art of Waging Peace* (2013).

Chenoweth, Erica, and Maria J. Stephan, *Why Civil Resistance Works: The Strategic Logic of Nonviolent Conflict* (2011).

Cortright, David, *Peace. A History of Movements and ideas* (2008).

Delgado, Sharon, *Shaking the Gates of Hell: Faith-led Resistance to Corporate Globalization* (2007).

Dower, John W., *Cultures of War: Pearl Harbor / Hiroshima / 9-11 / Iraq* (2010).

Faure-Brac, Russell, *Transition to Peace: A Defense Engineer's Search for an Alternative to War* (2012).

Fry, Douglas, *War, peace, and human nature: the convergence of evolutionary and cultural views* (2013).

Galtung, Johan. *Abolishing War. Criminalizing War, Removing War Causes, Removing War as Institution* (accessed 2016).

Galtung, Johan. *A Theory Of Peace. Building Direct-Structural-Cultural Peace* (accessed 2016).

Goldstein, Joshua S., *Winning the War on War: The Decline of Armed Conflict Worldwide* (2011).

Grossman, Dave, *On Killing: The Psychological Cost of Learning to Kill in War and Society* (1996).

Hand, Judith L., *Shift: The Beginning of War, the Ending of War* (2014).

Harris, Ian, and Mary Lee Morrison, *Peace Education, 3rd ed.,* (2012).

Hartsough, David, *Waging Peace: Global Adventures of a Lifelong Activist* (2014).

Hastings, Tom, *Ecology of War and Peace: Counting Costs of Conflict* (2000).

Hastings, Tom, *A New Era of Nonviolence. The Power of Civil Society over War* (2014).

Hawken, Paul, *Blessed Unrest: How the Largest Movement in the World Came into Being and Why No One Saw It Coming* (2007).

Irwin, Robert A., *Building a Peace System* (1989; free online via HathiTrust).

Kaldor, Mary, *Global Civil Society: An Answer to War* (2003).

Kelly, Kathy, *Other Lands Have Dreams: From Baghdad to Pekin Prison* (2005).

Lederach, John Paul, *The Moral Imagination: The Art and Soul of Building Peace* (2005).

Mahoney, Liam, and Luis Enrique Eguren, *Unarmed Bodyguards: International Accompaniment for the Protection of Human Rights* (1997).

Marr, Andrew, *Tools for Peace: The Spiritual Craft of St. Benedict and Rene Girard* (2007).

Mische, Patricia M., and Melissa Merkling, eds., *Toward a Global Civilization? The Contribution of Religions* (2001).

Myers, Winslow, *Living Beyond War. A Citizen's Guide* (2009).

Nagler, Michael, *The Search for a Nonviolent Future* (2004).

Nelson-Pallmeyer, Jack, *Authentic Hope: It's the End of the World As We Know It But Soft Landings Are Possible* (2012).

O'Dea, James, *Cultivating Peace: Becoming a 21st-Century Peace Ambassador* (2012).

Ricigliano, Rob, *Making Peace Last: A Toolbox for Sustainable Peacebuilding* (2012).

Schwartzberg, Joseph E., *Transforming the United Nations System* (2013).

Sharp, Gene, *Waging Nonviolent Struggle* (2005),

Sharp, Gene, *The Politics of nonviolent Action* (1973)

Sharp, Gene, *Civilian-Based Defense: A Post-Military Weapons System* (1990) available at http://www.aeinstein.org/wp-content/up-loads/2013/09/Civilian-Based-Defense-English.pdf

Shierd, Kent, *From War to Peace: A Guide to the Next Hundred Years* (2011).

Solomon, Norman. *War Made Easy: How Presidents and Pundits Keep Spinning Us to Death*. (2010)

Somlai, Anton, *Peace Vigil: Living Without Hesitation* (2009).

Swanson, David, *War No More: The Case for Abolition* (2013).

Swanson, David, *When the World Outlawed War* (2011).

Swanson, David, *War is a Lie* (2nd Ed., 2016).

Thompson, J. Milburn, *Justice & Peace: A Christian Primer* (2003).

Williams, Jody, Goose, Stephen., & Wareham, Mary. *Banning landmines: disarmament, citizen diplomacy, and human security* (2008).

Movies

A Bold Peace
A Force More Powerful
Bringing Down a Dictator
Orange Revolution
Pray the Devil Back to Hell
Paying the Price of Peace

A Sampling of other Peace Organizations on the World Wide Web

Albert Einstein Institution, www.aeinstein.org

American Friends Service Committee, www.afsc.org

Campaign to Close All Military Bases, www.tni.org/primer/foreign-military-bases-and-global-campaign-close-them

Campaign Nonviolence, www.paceebene.org/programs/campaign-nonviolence

Carter Center, www.cartercenter.org/peace/index.html

Christian Peacemaker Teams, www.cpt.org

Citizens for Global Solutions, www.globalsolutions.org

Conflict Resolution Center International, www.conflictres.org

Carnegie Endowment for International Peace, www.carnegieendowment.org

Coalition For Peace Action, www.peacecoalition.org/campaigns/peace-economy.html

Coalition for the International Criminal Court, www.iccnow.org

CodePink, www.codepink.org

Fellowship Of Reconciliation, www.forusa.org

Greenpeace, www.greenpeace.org

Hague Appeal For Peace, www.haguepeace.org

Human Rights Watch, www.hrw.org

Institute for Inclusive Security, www.inclusivesecurity.org

Institute for Multi-Track Diplomacy, www.imtd.org

International Center for Nonviolent Conflict, www.nonviolent-conflict.org

International Civil Society Action Network, http://www.icanpeacework.org

International Fellowship of Reconciliation, www.ifor.org

International Peace Research Association, www.iprapeace.org

International Peace Bureau, www.ipb.org

International Network for the Abolition of Foreign Military Bases, www.causes.com/nobases

Jewish Peace Fellowship, www.jewishpeacefellowship.org

Meiklejohn Civil Liberties Institute, www.mcli.org

Metta Center for Nonviolence, www.mettacenter.org

Muslim Peacemaker Teams Iraq, www.mpt-iraq.org

National Peace Foundation, www.nationalpeace.org

Nobel Women's Initiative, www.nobelwomensinitiative.com

Nonviolence International, www.nonviolenceinternational.net

Nonviolent Peaceforce, www.nonviolentpeaceforce.org

Nukewatch, www.nukewatch.com

Oxfam International, www.oxfam.org

Pace e Bene, www.paceebene.org

Peace Action Training and Research Institute of Romania (PATRIR), www.patrir.ro/en

Pax Christi, www.paxchristiusa.org

Peace Action, www.peace-action.org

Peace Brigades International, www.peacebrigades.org

Peace And Justice Studies Association, www.peacejusticestudies.org

Peace Direct, www.peacedirect.org

Peace People, www.peacepeople.com

PeaceVoice, www.peacevoice.info

The People's Charter to Create a Nonviolent World, www.thepeoplesnonviolencecharter.wordpress.com

Ploughshares Fund, www.ploughshares.org

Rotarian Action Group for Peace, www.rotarianactiongroupforpeace.org

Transcend International, www.transcend.org

United for Peace and Justice, www.unitedforpeace.org

United Nations Association of the United States (UNA/USA), www.unausa.org

Veterans for Peace, www.veteransforpeace.org

Waging Nonviolence, www.wagingnonviolence.org

Women's Action for New Directions, www.wand.org

War Prevention Initiative, www.warpreventioninitiative.org

War Resisters League, www.warresisters.org

War Resisters International, www.wri-irg.org

Women's International League for Peace and freedom, www.wilpfinternational.org

World Federalist Movement, www.igp.org

World Parliament, www.worldparliament-gov.org/home

... and the many, many wonderful organizations we cannot list here. You are part of the movement to end all war. We are one!

Please Note this is a work in progress and will always be a living document. We invite any and all to comment, critique and help to improve it.

CPSIA information can be obtained
at www.ICGtesting.com
Printed in the USA
BVOW05s1235251016

465803BV00036B/68/P